Until Heaven Parts Us

Until Heaven Parts Us

Alyssa Patterson

To Chandler, my precious late husband. May the generations know how well I was loved by you.

I will proclaim the love of Christ that has bound up my broken heart, until heaven joins us once more.

Table of Contents

Foreword

I have always been a science fiction nerd. One of the common themes that pops up is time travel. We have always been intrigued about being able to jump into Marty McFly's DeLorean, the phone booth, the time machine, the quantum realm, or the space capsule and go back into another place and time. We often fantasize about where and when we would go back to in the timeline. Where and when would you go? A favorite memory that you have? The grassy knoll in Dallas, November 22, 1963? I usually say I would go back to the Galilee around 30 AD and find Jesus ministering. But what if we could go back and change something in the past? Would you go back to stop some terrorists before they changed the world on September 11, 2001? Perhaps.

If it were possible for me to go back in time, there are several pivotal moments I would like to go back and change. The point in time that sticks out most in my mind would be to go back to that fateful day in June when Chan Patterson lost his life on the water. I would do everything in my power to keep that tragic accident from taking place. However, no such invention exists. The only person who I am aware of that could be capable of time travel is God—none of us even come close. So, what do we do with what we have left?

To know Chan was to know a well-rounded man's man. He loved the outdoors, music, hard work, and God's Word. Our two families have been close for the last twelve or so years. His mom taught our kids in school. I was their pastor. His dad, Breck, is our church administrator. Chan knew how to fill a room just with his presence. One of his friends said it right: *"Chan made everyone feel like they mattered."*

A few years ago, I started hearing whispers of a young lady who had captured Chan's attention. When things began to get serious between them, I could see why. I told Chan he had way out-punted his coverage! He just smiled with his big grin in agreement and a verbal commitment to hang on to her. She was a beauty, godly, a reader, intelligent, and also a hard worker like Chan. I thought I was a pretty big fan of the works of C.S. Lewis; in pretty much any room that she walks in, no one knows more about the author's writings than she does. Chan popped the question. They asked me to officiate their wedding. I told him that it would be an honor and privilege.

They both pressed into pre-marital counseling with abandon. I heard her story of being introduced to Christ through an instructor at her dance studio. We cruised through all six sessions with truth, depth, a few tears, and laughter. I could honestly say I had not been this encouraged about a newlywed couple in all of my ministry. These two were going to set the world on fire together. As individuals, both of them were rebellious to an out-of-control, woke culture caving in on itself. Together? *"Two are better than one for they have a good return for their labor"* (Ecclesiastes 4:9 NASB). They had a kingdom mindset in regard to their home, church, and work. The wedding was beautiful, Christ-exalting, and fun. These two married with Jesus as their foundation and would build a home that would be an obnoxiously powerful lighthouse to an increasingly dark world for the generations to follow after ours.

I was so excited for the road God had laid before them. However, we learn to check our expectations at God's feet. The road laid before us is not what we often think it is.

On a Saturday evening three weeks after the wedding, I was outside finishing some yard work. I checked my phone to see that I missed Breck's phone call. His shaking voice wanted me to call him about an emergency that had just happened. The voice mail is still on my phone to this day. Moments like these are "before and after." You remember what life was like before. You know what it is like after.

The book you have before you is a lament. Alyssa has written *Until Heaven Parts Us* as an encouragement to continue to love God and those he has given to you without fear but with courage and life-changing purpose. Some of you may not have gone through much loss. Some may be in bone-crushing grief. This account will help you no matter where you are. It is not a question of if, but when.

Alyssa's account will help you to take the time to mourn. *"Blessed are those who mourn,"* Jesus said. *"For they shall be comforted."* But what if they never mourn? The opposite makes sense: if you never mourn, you will never be comforted. God wants you to know him as the God of comfort. One of those comforts is knowing that the God of all comfort is on his throne in control of all things while simultaneously being worshipped by those saints, like Chan, who have gone before us. Check out Revelation chapters four, five, seven, and ultimately, nineteen. We worship with the saints. When we look up to him in worship, we are joining with an uncounted number that we will soon be reunited with.

Until then, we can't jump into the DeLorean and have it take us back in time to change everything and spare us all the heartbreak. But what we can do is trust God each step of the way. Why? Because God's road for us is different from what we expect, but ultimately more glorious.

"The LORD gave and the LORD has taken away. Blessed be the name of the LORD." Job 1:21 NASB

—Joey Thompson

A Heart Full of Grief

If these petals could
whisper secrets
of stories heard
before
I'm sure they'd
tell you soft
and slow,
"To you my spirit now adorns."
And every moon that
comes to pass
I hear their mellow
plea,
"come back"
they whisper soft and
sweet,
"come back, just stay, and be."

Written summer '18

𝒯he golf cart slowly whirred up the gravel path, and I caught a glimpse of the boys lined up in their black suits. My heart raced; I knew you were among them. I took in a deep breath of the fresh mountain air and smiled at my daddy beside me. This was the moment I had dreamed of a million times over since meeting Chandler.

My daddy offered me his hand and helped me out of the side of the golf cart. He gave me his arm, and I inhaled another deep breath of the fresh mountain air. We reached the end of the gravel where it met the lush green grass, alive with summer, alive as we were that day, and I stopped.

"Stars and Butterflies," a soundtrack from my favorite movie, began to play, and I took my first steps down the aisle to meet Chandler who would become my husband on that perfect day in June.

Closing my eyes, I can remember his sweet smile and his perfectly handsome face as I read my vows to him, proudly promising this:

"I don't know what this life has in store for us, but I do know two things that will always be true: the faithfulness of our God, and my love for you."

I didn't realize how tightly I would need to cling to that first fact in the days to come and how much my love for Chandler and Jesus would explode in the weeks to follow.

Less than a month later, I climbed out of our car, my daddy offered me his arm again and led me into a dark, empty-for-a-moment high school auditorium. At the bottom of the stairs, at the end of the aisle, Chandler waited for me again.

This time I walked alone, letting go of my daddy's arm and running to embrace the American-Flag-covered casket that held the remains of my husband's sweet body. Flesh of my flesh, bone of my bones. The most precious part of me had been taken far, far too soon.

As the auditorium filled and overflowed to the gymnasium, I saw the same boys in the same black suits they had worn on our wedding day just a few weeks prior. I emptied myself of hugs and tears that day and was a shadow of myself in the weeks to come.

I can't believe I have come to write this kind of story. I always knew I would one day write a book, but I never imagined it would be like this. Growing up, I always had an admiration for books and stories. I once droned on to my dad about how amazing I thought it was that of the millions and billions of stories people have written through the ages, we all have had access to the same words and phrases, and when those same words and phrases are organized in a different way, a completely different story is told.

After years of reading and rereading books like *A Grief Observed* by C.S. Lewis and *A Severe Mercy* by Sheldon Vanauken, and even going so far as to call them my "favorite," I found myself the one sitting in the widow seat at just twenty-three years old after three weeks of marriage. Instead of reading about grief, I was the one grieving. Instead of admiring their honesty, and bravery to be so, it was my turn to get honest, and to be brave.

As children, we dream about the pages of our favorite storybooks coming to life. Girls imagine themselves being rescued by the knight in shining armor. Boys see themselves slaying the dragon. This was not the story I wanted to be drawn into. This dragon that was grief wasn't what I wanted to face. But in facing it, I found a rescuer who was far greater than I had previously imagined him to be.

After just three weeks of beautiful marriage, my husband Chandler lost his life in a horrible accident, and at twenty-three years old, after just becoming his wife, I was made his widow. Beside myself with grief, I wrestled with the pain. I sat in pools of tears and slobber of sloppy grief with the Lord, and for some time, sorrow became my home. Like a pair of comfortable slippers, I often found myself slipping into the comfort of sorrow in the early mourning.

I bargained with the Lord, telling him I would do anything to have Chandler back, and I waited anxiously for the pain to subside or for Chandler to just walk back through our front door. It had all just been an awful dream, right?

I vividly remember feeling that the sorrow would never end. I prayed for the pain to stop. But the pain didn't go away. It still hasn't. It never will. It has merely changed and will continue to as the years go by.

There is a massive crater left in the hearts of everyone who knew my Chandler. His death left mass casualties of joy in its wake.

In my first year of grief, I was carried through by the companionship and encouragement of many, the love of family and friends, an abundance of prayers uttered by people I'd never met, endless casseroles, and the new morning mercies of my Father in heaven. With the absence of any one of these things, but especially my faith, I am not certain I would be writing this book barely a year beyond his passing, much less functioning enough to make it out of bed.

I am forever grateful and indebted to the prayers that strangers prayed on my behalf, casseroles, and my sweet Jesus for carrying me so tenderly through the darkest time of my life.

In those hellish days after losing Chandler, I couldn't move, breathe, sleep, or bathe. What was the point anyway? I had no desire to eat—even water tasted bad.

But I was surprised at my desire to speak and to share time with the people I loved most. I had feared that my explosion of emotion would lead me to push the ones I loved the most away, but instead, I was drawn to them even more, leaning in. I am grateful for the precious moments I had with the ones who came alongside me in the earliest days of my grief.

It was in those earliest days of grief that I felt the presence of the Lord in the most tangible way I ever have. It would sit heavy in the room. It made the air feel thicker. His presence was tangible and overwhelmingly peaceful. All my life I knew Jesus would be present in my pain as my God, but I didn't understand just how far he'd go to be there until he met me in the midst of it all.

In struggling through the grief, I learned just how intimately he understands our pain and that he truly grieves with us. In those moments of drowning in my own sorrow, wondering if it would ever let up, he was with me.

Chandler's favorite Scripture became an ironic source of comfort to many in the time following his death. It goes like this:

> "The Lord is my Shepherd [to feed, to guide and to shield me], I shall not want. He lets me lie down in green pastures; He leads me beside the still and quiet waters. He refreshes and restores my soul (life); He leads me in the paths of righteousness for His name's sake. Even though

I walk through the [sunless] valley of the shadow of death, I fear no evil, for You are with me; Your rod [to protect] and Your staff [to guide], they comfort and console me. You prepare a table before me in the presence of my enemies. You have anointed and refreshed my head with oil; My cup overflows. Surely goodness and mercy and unfailing love shall follow me all the days of my life, And I shall dwell forever [throughout all my days] in the house and in the presence of the Lord." (Psalm 23 AMP)

It is a strange and special gift to know this Scripture with such intimacy. To feel him physically restore my strength and refresh my soul on the days I just couldn't will myself to get out of bed was a gift like none other. To know that he stood with me in the shadow of Chandler's death, comforting and consoling me, brought me peace that surpassed understanding.

I would surely trade the way I came to know the realities of these verses so well, but I am thankful that this Scripture is true and unchanging. I am thankful that we're promised he will refresh our soul, even in seasons when we feel like nothing can.

During the months after losing Chandler, I barely had enough spiritual stamina to pray for myself. But it was in those utterly shattered moments when I would cry out to God, just asking him to help me, when I would find it was in my brokenness that I was being made whole. The level of elaboration in our prayers doesn't correlate to the good work God will do with them. Our Father seeks an honest heart, and in that season, I knew I needed him more than anything. It was in my grief alone that I was able to identify my true deep need for God.

But to be honest, days came and went where I didn't feel so certain. I hope my honesty in these pages conveys my struggle with God on the days that I *did* wrestle with him. They were many. I knew him near, I felt his favor and provision, but there were days I just couldn't understand why this would happen to a man like Chandler and to a woman like me who had been patient and faithful for so long.

On the days and nights I wrestled with that question, I always landed back at the feet of eternity, with a promise that all things would be made new again. And so, I would take a deep breath, mop the sorrow off the floor, put my *whys* on the shelf, and trust in him. I learned that sometimes holding on to the whys is more exhausting than just letting them go and setting them free, accepting the fact that an answer may never come.

In seasons of grief, I often wavered between letting my wonderings go to God and grasping at straws for answers. We're convinced that if a "good enough" explanation as to why something so awful would happen to a pair so faithful could be provided that we'd somehow be okay with it, but I don't think that's true. There is no cost that would make losing Chandler "worth it." No reason why that would make us ache for him less. I am so grateful that in my seasons of battling the why, my God doesn't change.

I got lunch with a girlfriend today who's struggling to find peace regarding her own grief, and I reminded her, with an understanding smile, that the goodness of our God doesn't depend on our heart toward him or our willingness to accept the gift of peace. He doesn't change, and he is always good. He knows how we're feeling before we even know we will feel it. Psalm 139 says this best.

"Lord, you know everything there is to know about me. You perceive every movement of my heart and soul, and you understand my every thought before it even enters my mind. You are so intimately aware of me, Lord. You read my heart like an open book and you know all the words I'm about to speak before I even start a sentence! You know every step I will take before my journey even begins. You've gone into my future to prepare the way, and in kindness you follow behind me to spare me from the harm of my past. You have laid your hand on me! This is just too wonderful, deep, and incomprehensible! Your understanding of me brings me wonder and strength.

"Where could I go from your Spirit? Where could I run and hide from your face? If I go up to heaven, you're there! If I go down to the realm of the dead, you're there too! If I fly with wings into the shining dawn, you're there! If I fly into the radiant sunset, you're there waiting!

"Wherever I go, your hand will guide me; your strength will empower me. It's impossible to disappear from you or to ask the darkness to hide me, for your presence is everywhere, bringing light into my night. There is no such thing as darkness with you. The night, to you, is as bright as the day; there's no difference between the two." (Psalm 139:1–12 TPT)

There is no place we can hide from him. Not even in the depths of our anger and grief. Even there, he is waiting for us, just to love us. I have found my hope in knowing that nothing changes about God when I grieve honestly, and in doing so, I have learned how to grieve well and sit with the Lord while doing it. I knew that no matter what I was saying, sobbing, or screaming, he had already gone before me, able to handle whatever I threw his way.

In this journey through grief, I have learned to find comfort in the fact that this is, and always was, Plan A. It's an odd comfort to find some ounce of assurance that this was always supposed to be. God knew when Chandler's last day on Earth would be, and by divine design, he crossed our paths *just* in time to fall in love and become husband and wife before he would be called home to heaven.

I remember shortly after Chandler died, I stumbled upon a photo of myself in my father's toolbox, which is always left open in my parents' garage. Automotive oil and other sorts of workshop grime splattered parts of the photo of a six-year-old me with glasses, curly hair, and a hat made of balloons. Upon seeing the picture once more, after walking by it a million times, I was stopped dead in my tracks in front of the greasy toolbox. I whispered, "You poor sweet girl" under my breath, knowing that *even then*, these days were destined to be mine.

I was always meant to meet and love a beautiful man from the Northeast Georgia Mountains. He was always meant to tell me he was going to marry me on our first date. I was always supposed to be Chandler's wife. And I was always meant to be his widow.

My prayer is that you find hope in the pages to come. Though this story is solemn and, to be frank, downright rotten, I hope you come to learn that God is still good, even in the sorrow.

A Touch of Heaven

"It's a heart"
she said so softly,
you could barely hear her pray:
"One like this. Oh please my God,
give me one someday."
She thought back to the months:
October,
June,
and May.
"My heart, Oh God has loved you still,
when all the seasons change."

Written fall '18

*S*ince I was a young girl in glasses, I had dreamed not only of my wedding day, like most little girls do, but even more of actually being married. I had dreamed of all the things that would come after I'd say "I do." I looked forward to being a wife and to loving my husband. I looked forward to making a house a home and having lots and lots of babies to fill up every room. And I especially looked forward to raising them to be people who loved the Lord with all their hearts with the man I loved beyond measure by my side.

I remember one moment where this dream of mine was affirmed so sweetly by the Lord, years before I met Chandler. I can't remember why I was out or where I was going, but I do remember pulling into the parking spot of my destination and feeling the weight of that long-awaited desire hit my stomach like a ton of bricks. The Lord made it crystal clear at that moment as he spoke to my heart that my calling would come once I got married.

So, naturally, I assumed that meant being a good and loving wife and raising lots and lots of babies to love the Lord with all their hearts.

Since Chandler's passing, I've recalled that memory often. A few times I have closed my eyes and put myself back in that parking spot, reconciling with the painful irony of the days that befell me after our wedding day.

The day Chandler proposed was a completely perfect surprise. All my life I had every intention to be completely aware of when my husband-to-be would propose because I couldn't stand the thought of being surprised. But Chandler was special, and he sure had me fooled.

It rained all morning and afternoon that day. On-and-off storm clouds covered the sky dressed in deep gray, and I was completely unassuming. Meanwhile, my sweet Chandler was pleading with God and the sky that the rain would let up when it came time for him to get down on one knee.

Later that evening, after finishing a meal with our sweet friends Brad and Macy, we climbed in the car and the boys both nodded at each other and turned back to us girls and said they had a surprise for us. Macy looked at me, shrugged her shoulders, and shook her head in a "What are they up to now?" kind of way, and we rode off over the mountain to South Carolina. Jason Aldean blasted through the car, and the music poured out the window, covering the wind with the simple joys of summer. It was a special kind of happiness you feel when everything is just right and no one is worried about clocking in to work the next morning. We were unbridled with happiness, undone with joy.

After a ten-minute ride, the boys pulled the car to the side of the road and jumped out to blindfold Macy and I, which caught me by surprise. I began to wonder what these two were up to. Once my blindfold was secured, Macy removed hers sneakily. I was sitting in the car that was overflowing with the scent of summer, filled with music and joy, completely oblivious to everything that was about to unfold. Eventually, the car rolled to a stop, and my heart began to race. The hope of a proposal rose up in my heart. I knew he and I both wanted our families to be part of our engagement and I knew we didn't have plans to be with them that day…but he sure did.

Chandler's rough, callused hand found mine and helped me out of the car. I could tell he was walking anxiously as he pulled me along, although I couldn't see a thing. As we walked, I was pushing down any hope of a proposal just in case the surprise was something completely different, like a sunset and a bottle of wine, which would have been perfect in its own right, but I couldn't help but hope. He was the man I wanted to spend all my days with. I wanted to have his babies and love him until *my* last breath.

As we turned a corner, "Dawn" from the Pride and Prejudice soundtrack filled the warm summer air, and I grabbed the top of his muscular shoulder and whispered "Babe?" as my heartbeat quickened.

His hands held me around my waist, and he placed me in the center of the outdoor venue. I couldn't see a thing, but I felt everything: his strong arms guiding me, the sweet music playing, and the summer wind warm. He removed my blindfold, and standing in front of me was our whole family, and a few sweet friends.

I gasped, as tears filled my eyes and thought in shock and disbelief, *This is really happening!*

I looked over my shoulder to find Chandler, the man of my dreams, down on one knee, and I was so enamored with what was about to take place that I hadn't noticed the beautiful array of flower arrangements and candles that decorated the venue. He held my waist in one strong hand and a beautiful ring in the other. It was perfect. He was so beautiful.

Chandler looked up at me with tears barely breaking over his beautiful blue eyes, and I touched his sweet clean-shaven face. He said, "I've loved you from the moment I met you. I want to spend forever with you, till death do us part. Will you marry me?"

I bet you can guess my answer…I let out a squeal and a "Yes!" and threw my arms around his neck as he stood to hold me.

We embraced for what felt like forever, and if I could have frozen time, I would have just held him there in that heavenly moment until the end of time. When I finally opened my eyes, I noticed the sky, which had stayed gray all day, had turned every shade of cotton candy, lavender, and citrus sorbet, and the vineyard below stretched on for miles and miles till they kissed the Blue Ridge Mountains in the great beyond.

I took a deep breath, kissed him, and thought, *Now this is heaven.*

In the weeks following our engagement, I received beautiful photos our lovely friend Marissa had taken of that most precious day. I wanted to memorialize those photos in a unique way, so I laid out the photos like a magazine with a headline that read "She Said Yes!"

This was big news! I was so proud to be his, and I was so eager to take his last name.

So I went to work sorting through each of the beautiful photos. As I relived that precious day, I stumbled upon a photo that was so unlike the rest. Marissa had snapped a picture as I reached my ballerina hand to touch his, hard worked and well loved. I thought about the photo as I admired his sweet hand reaching toward mine.

As I examined the reach to him, a feeling of separation dawned on me. That we'd be together for years and years to come "till death do us part" just like he had said in his proposal. When I completely filled in all the places for photos and text in our custom engagement magazine, I decided to add a last-minute, final touch. On the back of the magazine, I typed in red letters, "until heaven parts us," acknowledging an inevitable separation and a moving forward to be with our Father in heaven I was certain would happen when we'd gotten good and old.

Little did I know that less than a year from the printing of that engagement magazine, just three weeks after promising to be his faithful bride until heaven parted us, that very specific wedding vow would be made complete.

The *Creazione di Adamo* painted by Michelangelo lives on the ceiling of the Sistine Chapel and has been there since its completion in 1512. When I was just fifteen years old, I saw this painting with my very own eyes on a family vacation to Rome. I admired the wonder of a piece so grand and did my best to ignore the heavily armed Vatican police at every corner. Dumbfounded, I stared at the intricate artwork, older than anything I had ever seen, but all the more beautiful. The beauty had been preserved, along with the integrity of such immaculate artwork, seemingly frozen in time for years and years and years.

I stood with my eyes wide open—and my jaw too, most likely.

I stared at them, Adam and God. I looked at them, back and forth. Adam reaching out to God, God reaching out to Adam.

The photo of our hands almost touching at our engagement always reminded me of this artwork. The images both seem to me like yearning. The created's ache to spend forever with their Creator. The lovers ache to be together forever with their beloved. There is debate about the *Creazione di Adamo* being a coming together or separation between the Father and Adam. Were they meeting or parting? Was it beginning or end?

Separation is an inevitable fact of life, for all of us. In sin and in death. The thing, the hopeful thing, is that neither separation is permanent from our Creator or the ones we love. In salvation, we're reunited to both in eternity. The creation reunited forever with the Creator. The lover together again with the beloved.

The day we got engaged was covered in the whispers of heaven and that photo of our hands captured all that was to come so perfectly. To be parted, but to be rejoined again.

And now when I see that picture, I wonder, *Were we saying goodbye, or was he welcoming me home?*

From the sky to the proposal to the man, everything about that day held eternity at the heart. And I am so thankful, looking back on that wonderfully perfect day, that it was so.

Heaven touched down that day and continued to do so in incredible ways that blessed us so greatly in those months leading up to our marriage. And it is no wonder our God so lovingly reaches down on the extraordinary days, but it is an even sweeter gift when he sends this kind of beauty in the midst of the ordinary.

I can recall many small moments as Chandler and I were growing in love when I would just admire him from afar in wonder that such a man would be mine to love and cherish. There it would lie in a glance or conversation, a perfect touch of heaven reminding me this love was a precious gift which so greatly reflected the eternal love of Christ. A small glimpse of

Jesus's love for his bride, the church, had made itself a home in our very own love.

I have a video of Chandler on my Google Photos drive of him making us dinner with the song "It's a Great Day to Be Alive" by Travis Tritt playing in the background. I looked at him with wonder from where I sat on that normal afternoon and was so ready to give him my whole heart, for my whole life, and all the babies we could handle. And so, heaven touched down on that ordinary evening too, with a full heart and forever to go.

I am eternally grateful for these little moments. They are some of my favorite memories simply because they're magical and surprising. These little moments are often the ones that stack up over the years and shock us later when we remember something so seemingly regular. But isn't that the beauty of life? That the regular, the ordinary, and the mundane can be so intertwined, and that they can be embraced even more so with the gift of eternity always at the helm.

As these moments, big and small, passed me by, I never once stopped to wonder why they felt so complete and perfect. I was just grateful such a day would be mine. Looking back though, I realize all of that sweetness and fulfillment was but a shadow of the sweetness and fulfillment Chandler would be experiencing in eternity with Jesus. It is a sweetness and completion we all have the opportunity to experience one day. Like a bridegroom coming home to his bride, so we will be coming home to Christ.

1 Corinthians 13:12–13 paints a beautiful picture of our life now, compared to our *true life* with Christ in eternity. The writer points out that "until then" or "until heaven parts us" these things remain...

"For now we see but a faint reflection of riddles and mysteries as though reflected in a mirror, but one day we will see face-to-face. My understanding is incomplete now, but one day I will understand everything, just as everything about me has been fully understood. Until then, there are three things that remain: faith, hope, and love—yet love surpasses them all. So above all else, let love be the beautiful prize for which you run." (1 Corinthians 13:12–13 TPT)

All those years ago, sitting in the parking lot, stuck with the weight of my calling in my stomach, I now surely know this was meant for me. My story was to always proclaim that love is the beautiful prize for which we're called to run. To love your parents, to honor your spouse, to draw near to those seeking refuge, and in doing so point them to the lover of us all, Jesus Christ.

How beautiful it is that this life can reflect the beauties of eternity, in the quiet of a winter snow, or the first breath of morning light. And how much more beautiful is it that our earthly home is just a shadow of eternity. A faint reflection of riddles and mysteries. My understanding is incomplete now, but one day, one day, I will understand everything.

Grief & Gratitude

"Your Bride"
I dare not dream alone,
to fight to build a home.
For a woman who builds
one on wisdom,
will always fight for
The Kingdom.
And by her side,
will stand her dream
brought to life,
humble yet with pride.
Soft and ever still
she will be your bride.

Written fall '18

$\mathcal{M}$y eyes shot open at 4:00 a.m. that day. I had spent the majority of the night turning back and forth and back and forth until I finally couldn't take it anymore. I rolled over and whispered to my little sister, "Are you awake?" And like two little kids on Christmas, she rolled over to face me and said, "I can't sleep either." We got up, giggling, as we did often, and tiptoed into my parents' room just beside ours, and like we were little girls again, we crawled up onto the foot of their bed whispering for them to wake up, although they already were.

The morning buzzed with joy and mimosas. My friends and I all bounced around the room taking turns curling each other's hair, sipping coffee, and taking pictures. Our out-of-state guests stopped by the room occasionally throughout the morning to visit the bride. It was such a beautiful feeling to have all the people I loved the most in one place. I was on cloud nine, and I felt as cool as a cucumber. I did not spend a moment that day worrying over silly details or nervously awaiting seeing Chandler for the first time. I just couldn't wait to be his wife, and to give him a kiss, and to keep on kissing him for a long, long time…

When the music started and the people stood as I walked down the aisle toward Chandler, I felt like I could have run to him in that moment. As I got closer, I watched his sweet eyes fill with tears again, just like they did the day we got engaged. I remember my daddy passing my hand to him and me standing to face Chandler and thinking, *This is it!* I had prayed for this day long before I knew him, and we prayed together about this day and this journey since we met. That day was the fruition of so many prayers and so much planning, finally unfolding in the most beautiful way before us.

I was so taken up with love for him on that day. It was the actualization of a moment that had taken place a few years before, standing beside his red Tacoma at the much-dreaded end of our very first date when he took a step back admiring me in the parking lot light and said with such assurance, "I'm gonna marry you." This was the day his sweet promise and our perfect dream came true.

I was elated. I felt grown, and I was so ready to take on all of life's challenges with him by my side. Who could have imagined I would be facing my greatest challenge without him just weeks after we were married?

Chandler and I chose to write our own personal vows in addition to reciting the traditional ones. I am so grateful now that we had both. His sweet rich voice speaking the words "till death do us part" became too true and prophetic in the weeks that followed. In my personal vows to him, I said, "I don't know what this life has in store for us, but I do know two things that will always be true: the faithfulness of our God, and my love for you," and every word of that was true.

During the ceremony, the pastor who married us, Joey, incorporated some of my favorite C.S. Lewis quotes. These few turned out to point straight at heaven on that perfect June day.

One quote he shared at the end of the ceremony went like this:

"There are far, far better things ahead than any we leave behind."[1] For years I had read this quote like "the best is yet to come," but I had a friend remind me once that it actually points as far as we can go, to eternity, our life in heaven with Jesus being the ultimate good and perfect gift.

This next quote by Lewis is one of my all-time favorites and was also used in our wedding ceremony. In fact, the morning of our wedding, Joey texted me to make sure I actually wanted the quote to be used. I thought it odd, and in the hustle and bustle of my day I didn't respond. Of course, I wanted it used…it was my favorite.

"Appreciative love gazes and holds its breath and is silent, rejoices that such a wonder should exist even if not for him, will not be wholly dejected by losing her, would rather have it so than never to have seen her at all."[2]

I had never read the quote this way until after Chandler passed. Now, the quote reminds me of all those "regular" days I had spent admiring Chandler from across the room or while he slept, holding my breath, silent, rejoicing that such a wonder like him should exist, and for me, too!

I felt like the luckiest girl in the world. Even though we didn't grow old together, I am so thankful I was the one who got to be his bride and had the honor of taking his last name. I am ever grateful to have loved him even though I lost him. Ever grateful to have known him than to never have met him at all.

That is the beauty of true gratitude, the courage of real love, and the price you pay when grief comes crashing down. To know truly, that the Lord holds us all in the palm of his hand and, in the meantime, we have the chance to love someone so much that even in the grief and pain, we find ourselves grateful. Grateful to have loved such a one. Grateful to have known them. Grateful to have called them our very own.

Our wedding day was a day of so many lasts, and so many firsts, which my sweet daddy spoke of in his speech. It was the last time I'd be crawling in bed with my parents giggling with excitement. It would be the first time Chandler could call me his wife, and not only for pretend. The last time I would bear my maiden name, and the first time I would take a new name.

In his speech, my dad shared this, and it has rung in our hearts ever since that beautiful day:

"From the moment you hold your baby in your arms, you find a new meaning of true love and responsibility. You'll never be ready for that most special moment and never be the same.

"You will come to know tiredness like you never knew it before. Days will run into days that are exactly the same, feedings, diaper changes, and yes, crying. Whining, fighting, naps—or lack of naps—it may at times seem like a never-ending cycle.

"But don't forget, there is a last time for everything. There will come a time when you will feed your baby for the very last time. They will fall asleep on you, and it will be the last time you ever hold your sleeping child. One day you will carry them on your hip then set them down, and never pick them up that way again. They will hold your hand to cross the road then never reach for it again. They will creep into your room at midnight for cuddles, and it will be the last night you ever wake to this.

"One afternoon you will sing 'The Wheels on the Bus' and do all the actions, then never sing them that song again. They will kiss you goodbye at the school gate, and the next day they will ask to walk to the gate alone. You will read your last bedtime story and wipe your last dirty face. They will run to you, arms raised, for the very last time.

"The thing is you won't even know it's the last time until there are no more times, and even then, it will take you a while to realize it. So, while you are living in these times, remember there are only so many of them, and when they are gone, you will yearn for just one more day—for one last time."

This was, and remains, a timely reminder, as we were all about to be experiencing more lasts than we knew. More lasts than anyone could have prepared for. It is a wonder those are the words that my dad chose to speak that day, but I am so glad he did. It was as if his spirit, through the Holy Spirit, had gone before him to prepare us for the grief and all of the lasts that were coming.

The small bit of life I shared with Chandler here on this Earth was such a good and perfect gift, and I am grateful for every single moment we shared, and while I would trade all I own and more to have loved him for so much longer, to fight in the kitchen, to fall asleep laughing, to go to church on Sundays, I stand by this when I say it, that I would do it all again, even knowing what I do now because knowing him, loving him, and being his bride has been worth every single tear-soaked late night I have spent in the shadow of grief since losing him.

"If you, imperfect as you are, know how to lovingly take care of your children and give them what's best, how much more ready is your heavenly Father to give wonderful gifts to those who ask him?" (Matthew 7:11 TPT)

Our wedding day was that wonderful gift. In hindsight, it is even more special that the days that were numbered for Chandler included our happiest, most precious memory. I am so grateful we got that day and that he was able to experience the joy of celebrating our marriage and was able to see the beauty of everyone who loved us most in the world dancing beneath a firefly-lit sky, champagne in hand, on that perfect day in June.

I had everything to be grateful for. I had an incredible husband who was the most hardworking, handsome, tenderhearted, strong-willed, confident yet humble man I ever knew. I had parents and a sister who loved me. I even had new parents and a new sister who loved me too! We had amazing family and friends who showed up and showed out to celebrate our union. And in the blessings upon a billion blessings, my grief and my gratitude became good friends.

The perfect day in June, the perfect dress, and perfect suit. The most beautiful flowers, all thanks to my momma. The yummiest cake and all of the champagne a bride could dream of. It was truly perfect, and without the help of my momma in those days, months, and weeks leading up to the big day, it wouldn't have been nearly so.

Because of my great, overwhelming gratitude, in the weeks to come, I would see grief rear its ugly head in the wake of Chandler's death. We weren't perfect by any means, but being biased, I would say we were an excellent match, one made in heaven, you might say.

Having gone from the highest of highs to the lowest of lows in such a short period of time was such a roller coaster, and still is. But on that wild ride, it forced me to cling to the Lord even harder in the days that were waiting for me, just a honeymoon and a couple of weeks away.

Chandler loved me the way every woman deserves to be loved. He fought for me, prayed with me and for me, and made me laugh till I cried. He held me in those strong, safe arms, and I knew I was forever his girl. He was passionate. He was kind. He loved me with such sweetness. A girl's dream. He was my favorite answered prayer that I had fought for, and stood faithfully by, for years.

I felt so thankful I could now relax into the blessing, and relish in the beauty of my groom. But I wasn't prepared for it to end as abruptly as it did, as I had just begun to find comfort, and rest, in the good gift of having Chandler as my husband. As soon as I had time to unpack from the honeymoon and settle my spirit beside the warmth of him every night, he was taken up to heaven.

I'm thankful still that I had so much to be grateful for, the perfect groom, and the most precious wedding day. I am thankful I have so much to miss. Not everyone is so lucky to be loved so well. I struck gold when I fell in love with Chandler, which has only made the grief more painful.

Great love will always mean great loss when death swings low. For *this* is what the good Lord meant when he said, "Blessed are those who mourn" (Matthew 5:4). He gives good gifts, and as a result, we grieve those good gifts when separation comes. No one can evade death, but we can all embrace the gift that is love. And what a gift it can be when it is tethered to Christ.

A Golden Road

I think often of spring;
and always of you.
If one thing is sure,
and entirely true
it's that:
If they chase the sun,
their freedom will never
set with it
& the wild inside them
rises with every new dawn.

Written summer '18

A few weeks before our wedding, Chandler and I found what we would call our "church home." A precious church, led by a humble and fierce leader, and filled with all walks of life, just a ten-minute ride from our beautiful new home.

Our first time attending, we admittedly arrived a few minutes late, and slid into seats in the back row which was mostly empty. It was such a gift to be able to worship beside the man who would become my husband in only a few more Sundays. I embraced that gift and stood close beside him the whole time, holding his hand tight in awe that he was mine for the taking and that we'd get to spend the rest of our Sundays together, in common community, worshipping our Father in heaven, just like this.

When worship closed in prayer, we sat for the teaching. We held hands, his resting under mine in his lap. The pastor began to lead us in a teaching on baptism. I had been christened as a baby and saved as a young girl but had not been baptized by my own conviction, and I knew it was something I needed to do as an outward proclamation of my faith. After many years of moving often, I had never felt fully at home with a church family, until this day.

I remember feeling the pull to be obedient and say "Yes!" to this call when our pastor began to describe baptism as a wedding ring being an outward sign of our commitment to our faith just like a wedding ring is the example of our outward commitment to our spouse. Being just a few weeks away from our very own wedding day, I knew this was the perfect time and place. Our pastor closed his teaching and we stood again to worship, Chandler and I still attached at the hip. I felt my eyes burn with tears as I squeezed Chandler's hand. I leaned over to him and said, "I want to get baptized." When he looked down at my tear-filled eyes, he hugged me tight and said, "Right now?" I giggled and said, "No, not right now, but soon."

After the service ended, we mingled our way through the crowd to introduce ourselves to Pastor Brian. Chandler let him know, with pride, that we were about to be married in a few weeks and we wanted to be plugged in everywhere we could. Chandler and I both felt called to serve. We wanted to join a newlywed small group and build a new community of our very own. We were all in!

When I told the pastor about my decision to be baptized and why his teaching was so relevant that day, he without hesitation took a slip of paper and asked me to write down my name and phone number. I scribbled my number down sloppily in excitement and handed it back to him. A few days later, we were coordinating my baptism for the weekend after we would return home from our honeymoon.

I would be a married woman, with a ring to symbolize my dedication to Chandler, and a baptism to symbolize my dedication to Jesus. My baptism was to be my marriage to my faith, proclaiming that I would stand my ground no matter what. Promising that I would stay in sickness, and in health. I would stand by Jesus's side, even in death, sorrow, and grief.

On Father's Day, June 20, 2021, Chandler and I, the new Mr. and Mrs. Patterson, climbed in our red Tacoma and took off to church with my change of clothes and Bible in hand. When we arrived at the church, we found our parents, our sisters, and his grandparents gathered together waiting on us. I kissed Chandler goodbye and changed into a shirt from the church that said "You Belong." I shuffled backstage and listened to the worship with butterflies filling my stomach. The same butterflies I had when I was just about to walk down the aisle to Chandler a couple of weekends before.

When they prayed over me and sent me to the stage, I climbed into those waters and was greatly relieved to find them warm. I answered a few questions with "I do" to proclaim my faith in Jesus, and after a dunk under the water, it was so.

Pastor Brian gave me a hug and proudly proclaimed that I was "fresh off a honeymoon" and the crowd, our family, and Chandler roared with *woohoos* and applause. As I walked back to my seat after changing out of my wet clothes, my hair still wet, Chandler embraced me in his giant, loving arms. I fit so perfectly on his chest, and he kissed me for quite a long time for being in church. He grabbed my face and softly whispered, "I am so proud of you."

At that moment I knew our love would grow in so many beautiful ways in each day to come, budding and blossoming out in every direction. He was proud of me at that moment, and I was just so proud to be his. I relished in the gift of being his bride and was in awe at all the goodness the Lord was lavishly pouring out in the simple gift of going to church and having Sunday lunch with our families. Two had truly become one.

That afternoon we hosted our first, of what should have been many, post-church Sunday lunches. Chandler grilled chicken thighs on the bar-b-que. My mom, mother-in-law, and both of our grandmothers shuffled around the kitchen helping me get things in order. We set out snacks, and the routine Sunday football game noise filled the house, on top of Chandler's music playing outside by the grill.

We all filled our bellies to the brim with bar-b-que, coleslaw, deviled eggs, and the like. We sipped sweet tea and enjoyed berry crisp cobbler with vanilla ice cream. The day and the weather, both warm.

Grandaddy fell asleep on the couch sitting straight up, and we giggled at his snore from afar. We were turning a page. We were one great big happy family. We were one. We were the hosts this time, in our own home too, and we were so proud.

Our parents stayed to help us clean, even though we insisted they not worry themselves with it. When the last dish was dried and put up, we waved our families goodbye at the front door holding onto each other. And when we shut the door behind them, I remember feeling like the cherry on top of the rest of my life was that, no matter what, he would be the one I would end my days with. We'd entertain and find joy in time spent sharing a meal and a memory with family and friends, and then when the dishes were dried, and the last glass of wine was drunk, it would always be the two of us at the end of every day.

And I wish with all my might that in that moment I had been right.

Like I said in my wedding vows weeks earlier, "I don't know what this life has in store for us, but I do know two things that will always be true: the faithfulness of our God, and my love for you." I had no idea how much that baptism and that day would come to teach me. That an act of obedience must be taken up as quickly as it is offered and that there is this hope as an anchor for our souls that goes far beyond what we can comprehend this side of heaven.

> "This hope [this confident assurance] we have as an anchor of the soul [it cannot slip and it cannot break down under whatever pressure bears upon it]—a safe and steadfast hope that enters within the veil [of the heavenly temple, that most Holy Place in which the very presence of God dwells]." (Hebrews 6:19 AMP)

On my baptism day, I was proclaiming to myself, my husband, my family, and to those who were part of my church family that my hope in Christ would be the anchor for my soul. No matter what. Just like in our wedding vows, we promised our fidelity to each other for better or for worse, for richer or poorer, in sickness and in health, to love and to cherish, till death do us part.

The same promises ring true to my fidelity to my sweet Jesus, the only thing that is different is that death will never part *us*. When I was baptized, I pledged my faith would stand, for better or for worse, for richer or poorer, in sickness and in health, and even if weathered by death, my faith would remain my stronghold.

It was only a week later that I was encountering death and everything it had taken from me head on.

I had made my choice to abide always. In the weeks to come, I encountered some days where it was so apparent that the Lord was drawing me nearer and nearer. I also faced days, and still do, where my anger swells and the sorrow steeps my soul, but God never changes. And that is why I am so thankful for the commitment that I made, because no matter how much I change, fail to believe, or find myself angry, he is always the same.

Jesus would simply always be waiting for me to come home, leaving the front porch light on and sleeping with one eye open, like a good Father does. He waits for his children. He sits with us in our fear, he rests with us in our gratitude, and he abides with us in our pain.

It is absolutely true that I didn't know what life had in store for us, or me, or him just that very next weekend. But *God did know*, and that baptism was a spiritual pre-game of sorts, readying me for what was just around the corner.

I have come to learn that as easy as it is to get caught up in the monotony of life, there is so much being orchestrated that we can't see, and couldn't possibly discover. This life is so much bigger than me and my happiness, and I surrender it before the Father, trusting that he will right every wrong in the light of eternity.

God knew what was just around the corner, and I believe he held Chandler and I so tenderly in that week to come. I imagine him holding us together in those sweet, but few, moments I shared with Chandler as my husband. Jesus watching us with admiration as his precious children who were so eager to do his work.

"You saw who you created me to be before I became me! Before I'd ever seen the light of day, the number of days you planned for me were already recorded in your book." (Psalm 139:16–18 TPT)

I have thought so much about my baptism since Chandler's accident. I am not sure I would have the courage now to be submerged. I am so grateful he was there to see me take that step in my faith journey as we were a newly married couple. I am so thankful I made the choice to be obedient when I felt the Lord drawing me toward him. There is no time to delay when you feel the calling to be obedient. Life is too short and fleeting not to do so. Urgency covers everything now.

While writing this book I have recalled several things I had written over the years that pointed towards heaven, even then. I wrote down this next passage in the fall of 2018 after having a recurrent vision:

I was running down a road, it was gold, and for a few months, that was all I saw: myself, hurtling down a street of gold. Later, as the vision developed, I found myself at the break of the ocean, which met the golden road, and on that ocean, I danced.

I hadn't thought about this vision or what it meant until today, and at the completion of my college career, I am gently reminded how important it is, even more so now, that I continue running down that road toward eternity. For if I know that eternity, for me, begins today. I am free to live the depth of every moment to its fullest—in laughter, in tears, in love, in war. To feel it, as far as the feeling goes, for we are fleeting and my voice will be heard.

A golden road that mirrors heaven and a vision of me dancing on the water and the waves—the very place my husband lost his life—daring Satan and all of hell to try and take my hope, as I let the Lord turn my mourning into dancing, all those years ago.

Last night I opened up to Revelation 21:18 and read onward about this city made of gold, the New Jerusalem, and smiled at the thought of me running down its roads, on toward the ocean and the sunset, dancing with the waves.

He surely tries, but Satan doesn't win. He does not get the last word. He does not get the final dance.

> "The wall was built of jasper; and the city was pure gold, transparent like clear crystal. The foundation stones of the wall of the city were adorned with every kind of precious stone. The first foundation stone was jasper; the second, sapphire; the third, chalcedony; the fourth, emerald; the fifth, sardonyx; the sixth, sardius; the seventh, chrysolite (yellow topaz); the eighth, beryl; the ninth, topaz; the tenth, chrysoprase; the eleventh, jacinth; the twelfth, amethyst. And the twelve gates were twelve pearls; each separate gate was of one single pearl. And the street (broad way) of the city was pure gold, like transparent crystal.

> "I saw no temple in it, for the Lord God Almighty [the Omnipotent, the Ruler of all] and the Lamb are its temple. And the city has no need of the sun nor of the moon to give light to it, for the glory (splendor, radiance) of God has illumined it, and the Lamb is its lamp and light. The nations [the redeemed people from the earth] will walk by its light, and the kings of the earth will bring into it their glory." (Revelation 21:18–24 AMP)

When Heaven
Parted Us

"Goodness & love are as real as their terrible opposites, and, in truth, far more real, though I say this mindful of the enormous evils…But love is the final reality; and anyone who does not understand this, be he writer or sage, is a man flawed of wisdom."

—Sheldon Vanauken, *A Severe Mercy: A Story of Faith, Tragedy and Triumph*

*H*e walked in from the end of his shift at the fire department that morning at around 8:30 a.m. and threw his duffle bag at the foot of the stairs to take up with him later. He had coffee and our favorite breakfast sandwiches from Dunkin' Donuts in hand. I welcomed him with a kiss.

We sat together, sipped our coffee, and ate our breakfast, and I asked him about his evening. He was tired. The night before had been a long shift, and he hadn't gotten much sleep, which wasn't unusual for him.

Since we had moved into the house, we (I) had started feeding the neighborhood cat. She was white with brown, brindle, and orange spots, and had piercing yellow eyes. The rainy Friday night before, I had set out an open can of tuna on the front porch, and the next morning I was elated to find that it had been emptied. I told Chandler about this exciting news, that I was luring the neighborhood stray to our home, and he chuckled at my level of excitement over an empty can of tuna. He proceeded to get up from the table and began to fill up a bowl with milk.

"Still hungry, going for cereal?" I asked him.

"No. I'm going to feed the cat." He smiled back at me.

I followed behind him like a child to our backyard where he slowly approached the cat that was just on the other side of our neighbor's property line. He set the bowl of milk down and backed up slowly to meet me. We waited for a few moments together, before the cat took off into the tree line. I didn't see her again after that day. Little did I know she wasn't the only one I'd be seeing for the very last time.

Chandler and I jumped in the car around 9:30 a.m. and headed to the campground where I would kiss him goodbye for the last time. The car was quiet. I am not much of a morning person, and he was still tired from last night's shift. We chatted about the week ahead and the trips we wanted to plan to go see friends. We stopped once for gas and continued on our way. So far, the day had been ordinary. Perfectly so.

We navigated to the campground he was meeting his buddies at, and we pulled to the side of a dirt road and waited for them there. While we waited, he pointed out the wild mountain ragweed to me, and I remember thinking he looked so adorable and youthful that day. So manly, but in spirit, he was just like a little boy.

After a few moments, enjoying the mountain summer air together, his buddies pulled up in a truck behind us, and they all hopped out and exchanged hugs. I gave him a quick kiss, so as to not draw too much attention in front of the boys. I hugged his buddy and told them "not to get in too much trouble" with a wink and a smile. I turned to leave, and I didn't look back.

It was just an ordinary day. The thought of never seeing him again after that moment wasn't even remotely on my radar.

As I drove back out of the campground, I decided to pull over beside a field of wildflowers that had caught my eye on the drive in. It reminded me very much of the way his sweet town looked the first time he showed me around. I plucked the flowers— deep crimson, orange, and bright yellow, all the happiest kinds of colors—until I had a bouquet. It was not quite as elaborate as the one I had carried down the aisle a few weeks before, but just as beautiful, and surely more wild.

Looking back now, I treasure that moment greatly. It was special because it was the last moment of pure beauty, peace, and solitude I would have for many, many months. I had flowers painted on my nails that day, I wore a summer blouse that was covered in wildflowers, and I proudly held my new bouquet that was so wild and alive.

I was covered in life. For a sweet summer moment, everything was blooming. Everything was growing.

I spent the day with my mother- and father-in-law. I sat in the kitchen with my mother-in-law and, in hindsight, we talked about silly things that were worrying us. We encouraged and comforted each other, and I am grateful to say that despite this tragedy, that hasn't changed. In fact, our relationship and bond has grown even closer. They are forever my family, just as my own blood.

That afternoon, as we headed up the road to make our way toward a family dinner, the phone rang. And how I wish it wouldn't have. Within moments of that call, we were turned around, hightailing it to the lake.

His mother cried out to the Lord in prayer, and I couldn't even muster an "Amen." I was frozen in shock and disbelief that I had just been robbed of my most perfect gift. Everything we had planned, every distant dream, came crashing down on top of me. My whole body shook. I couldn't say a word. I remembered wondering if I should I call my parents, knowing that if I did, it would immediately throw the whole moment into the horrific reality I was trying to deny.

I dialed the phone and said there had been an accident, and as soon as I spoke, they were on their way. I called several people, including my bridesmaids, asking them to pray. Some prayed with me on the line, for Chandler's safe return, but I knew that he was already gone.

Flesh of my flesh. Bone of my bones. We were two that had become one. I felt the instant separation in my soul that he was no longer earthside. No matter how many prayers would be prayed on my behalf that afternoon, and into the evening as they searched for my sweet husband's body, it was finished. And I knew it.

We eventually made our way down to the lake to join the Department of Natural Resources and the search effort. And to my horror, I found the aura of Chandler hanging in my midst. His presence had become tangible and was spread across the sky, absorbed into every molecule of summer mountain air. His spirit was playing with the breeze. His passing from life on earth to life in eternity was undoubtedly evident.

My soul was covered in misery. I wanted to crawl into a hole and just pass on to the next life myself, if only I could be with him. I ached to have him close. I buried my knees in the gravel for most of the time we spent at the lake that day, and as the sun sank, the searching paused for the evening.

I climbed into my parents' truck when the sky began to darken and let out a groan only deep grief can bring out of a human being. It was a sound I heard several times in the days to follow.

If you've heard the sound, you know. And if you haven't, you're blessed. Some of my first words as a widow after being a wife for only three weeks were not pleasant ones.

In the back of their truck, I screamed, "I'm twenty-three and I am a (choose your own curse word) widow?" As far as I was concerned, my life was over, surely the most lovely and beautiful parts.

My mom encouraged me with a tumbler of water on the car ride back to our home. The shock and the grief my body had been thrust into caused water to taste of sulfur. Now I think I know why. He lost his life on the water. How could I allow it to nourish mine?

For days I refused to drink because it tasted so awful.

I asked my mom, quite pointedly as we stopped for gas, "If it isn't about our happiness, then what are we even here for?" I knew the answer but wished that my life had been and always would be about me and my happiness, having him, and all the dreams we had planned to play out into our old age.

In those initial days, as Chandler's spirit fell thick around us, the Lord drew near to us as well. I felt his spirit hanging in the balance of every room, heavy with us, mourning with us, with the rumbling of redemption reverberating off every hug and held hand. There was a plan, bigger than our happiness. And it was already underway, and it was ours for the embracing.

Embracing that redemption plan comforted me greatly. And so, I knew that I too would be called to comfort those who would need comforting. It was a good lesson learned from my counselor in the weeks to come when I asked him the same question: "If it isn't about our happiness, then what are we even here for?"

So it wasn't about my happiness, and it isn't about yours. It's about how you and I would choose to glorify and rely on God in our sorrow, horror, and unhappiness. In the seasons until heaven parts us, how will you lean in? How will you abide?

"All praises belong to the God and Father of our Lord Jesus Christ. For he is the Father of tender mercy and the God of endless comfort. He always comes alongside us to comfort us in every suffering so that we can come alongside those who are in any painful trial. We can bring them this same comfort that God has poured out upon us. And just as we experience the abundance of Christ's own sufferings, even more of God's comfort will cascade upon us through our union with Christ." (2 Corinthians 1:3–5 TPT)

To be frank, I couldn't comfort anyone in those early days, but I knew even then that it wasn't just about my happiness or the joy we find on earth but multiplying our family in eternity through salvation. It was a humbling moment—realizing it isn't about me, not even a little bit. And I learned that lesson in a great big way that some, maybe most, never come to face—living the rest of their days serving only themselves. What an empty way to be.

I found great comfort in the months that followed in the Scripture that reminds us that the last shall be first. I didn't have to have it all together to approach our Father in prayer. And thank goodness. I was lucky most days if I had the appetite to eat all three meals and shower. It was a miracle the first day I was able to do both of those things.

I didn't have to be cleaned up emotionally or physically or be at peace to return to my Father. In fact, some of the moments I have felt most near to him were the nights I would cry out to him in anger, emotionally and physically spent, sometimes nearly cursing his name. I could feel his presence in my midst. He was holding my hand. He was waiting, he was listening, he was weeping right along with me.

He weeps with you too, in your sorrow and trial, and stands beside you even in your unbelief. You may feel like you're at the end of your rope, the last in line, but believe me when I say he is ever-present with you in that moment too. The last shall be first. "So those who are last [in this world] shall be first [in the world to come], and those who are first, last." (Matthew 20:16 AMP)

I didn't eat much else besides fruit and a saltine or two in that first week. Finally, something comforting caught my senses. Something that had been in my family cookbook for years. Every good Italian family has their signature spin on this dish...

I walked into the kitchen at my in-laws' home after making arrangements for Chandler's celebration of life. I felt drunk from the number of tears I had shed, and the beginning of a migraine pinched the back of my eyes. The house was filled with people, voices hushed, but the chattering continued when I entered. I was stopped by several hugs, but the scent of the sweet tomato sauce and bubbly parmesan cheese was making my stomach grumble. The feeling caught me by surprise.

I took a seat, and Katie, a childhood friend of Chandler's, handed me her baby. I felt the little one's sweet hand wrap around my finger and her two-tooth smile made one break on my face too. Her honest eyes locked on mine, reading me like a book. Before I could even ask, a large helping of Aunt Jeanne's lasagna was down on a plate in front of me. The room stopped as all watched in anticipation. I took a bite, it tasted delicious, it kind of tasted like home. My mom watched me eat the whole plate, and with every bite I took, she smiled.

I held that baby who made me smile for a moment, and I enjoyed the lasagna. Slowly, I was coming back to life myself. Slowly, but surely, hope was stirring.

Where the Red
Fern Grows

"Grief…gives life a permanently provisional feeling. It doesn't seem worth starting anything. I can't settle down. I yawn, I fidget, I smoke too much. Up till this I always had too little time. Now there is nothing but time. Almost pure time, empty successiveness."

—C.S. Lewis, *A Grief Observed*

C~ met him at the end of the aisle, of the quiet-for-a-moment
high school auditorium. On our wedding day he wore
American flag suspenders, and today his casket was covered in the
same Stars and Stripes. I had been dressed in white just a few weeks
before, and now I was covered in black from head to toe. How
could I have changed from a bridal gown to mourning clothes
so quickly, and for my groom too? Nothing made sense. It still
doesn't. I don't think it ever will.

I can only say I am grateful life isn't limited to my ability to
understand it.

On that sweltering day in July, I donned a black ankle-length
pleated skirt and a black quarter-sleeve top. I made my best attempt
to do my hair the same as it was on our wedding day. I'm not even
sure why I tried to put makeup on as I cried most of it off, and by
the end of the day, I had brushed out the curls in my hair.

I felt nauseous and nervous all morning. From the moment
I woke, I had been a shaky mess. I didn't eat anything that day
but one chicken mini from Chick-fil-A. Nothing is more of an
appetite killer than grief. Nothing like an appetite killer so much
as burying your husband of three short weeks.

So much rushed into my brain that morning as I brushed my
teeth, and I tried my best to manage my unwashed hair. Quotes
from books I had read played back in my mind over and over again.
The week I took in preparation for writing Chandler's eulogy led
me to some of the stories I loved most.

In the days in between Chandler's passing and his funeral, I
found a few spare moments to reference the stories I had always
admired. *A Grief Observed* was among them. I took out my well-read,
highlighted copy from my living room bookshelves and flipped

through its pages, still in disbelief that my story had come to so closely resemble that of Jack and Joy's.

I sat in the rocking chairs Chandler had just purchased for us the weekend before. He picked out a pillow with flowers on it for my chair that said "Welcome Home," and he chose a pillow with a red pickup truck and a retriever on the tailgate for his.

I took a seat in mine with a glass of sweet tea in hand, and for a few seconds, I closed my eyes. I wasn't tired. I didn't need to rest. It just felt like maybe for a moment I could just pretend like everything was normal, like he'd be coming back home from a long hard day any minute now. I would make supper, light a candle or two, and we'd enjoy a glass of white wine and one another. After a few moments of pretending, my eyes shot open, burning with tears once more at my reality. I wasn't waiting for him to come home. I was writing his eulogy.

Shaken back to my task at hand, I flipped through the book's worn pages, and one quote I had highlighted bright yellow stood out from the rest. It met me right where I was.

"No one ever told me that grief felt so like fear. I am not afraid, but the sensation is like being afraid. The same fluttering in the stomach, the same restlessness, the yawning. I keep on swallowing. At other times it feels like being mildly drunk, or concussed. There is a sort of invisible blanket between the world and me. I find it hard to take in what anyone says. Or perhaps, hard to want to take it in. It is so uninteresting. Yet I want the others to be about me. I dread the moments when the house is empty. If only they would talk to one another and not to me."[3]

A Grief Observed was a book I read for the first time at eighteen years old. Today, at twenty-three, it was hitting way too close to home. Lewis had been widowed at sixty-two after about three years of covenant marriage to his Joy, and I was widowed at twenty-three, after just three weeks of being married to my Chandler. Nothing was as it should be. For death never is "as it should be" because we weren't created for it to begin with.

I flipped through the pages of several other stories on that summer day and dumped the best words I could scramble together on my phone and prayed it would do Chandler, and the love we shared, justice.

When we arrived at the auditorium, we were almost immediately assigned our standing order in front of Chandler's casket. People flooded the room the moment the doors were opened for guests, and they just kept on coming.

After hugging people for hours, with his American-flag-covered casket and the man posting guard just behind us, we were ushered out of the auditorium. I was relieved to have a few moments that didn't include an "I'm sorry for your loss" and a sad smile. If I'd had the energy, I would have run over the top of the mountain behind the school and hid somewhere just to be alone with the wind and Chandler.

I shoved a chicken mini in my mouth and forced myself to swallow it down, and after a few moments, the funeral director entered the room and lined us up again. We processed into the auditorium to the song "A Rock" by Hardy, and when the song stopped, we all sat. We listened to some more music in true Chandler fashion, and people even stood and clapped along to "Huntin', Fishin', and Lovin' Every Day" by Luke Bryan. I just stood and cried while laughing at the ridiculousness of it all, tears washing away every ounce of makeup I had applied.

After Joey, who had married us just a few weeks prior, said a few words, it was my turn to speak. After Chandler went on to heaven, I knew immediately that I would need to put on my big girl pants and pull myself up by the bootstraps for this one. I loved him more than anything on this earth, and I took it up as my new responsibility as his wife and his widow to love him and honor him as best I could in this new and horrid condition.

I know without a doubt that if the roles were reversed, he would have eulogized me, and so I knew I had to speak for him. Being one who's always loved words, I knew it would bring me peace and comfort to write something of a final goodbye to him. I now treasure it as some of my best, most honest writing.

I walked past his casket, stepped behind the podium, and took a deep breath. As I looked out on the crowd of thousands, I giggled while my eyes stung with tears. I am sure that laughter wasn't the first thing the crowd full of mourning folk were expecting out of me, but to be fair, I hadn't expected it either. It wasn't anything that resembled joyful laughter, but more of a huff of disbelief at what I was about to say and why I was saying it.

Though it brought me great pride to be the wife of a man who could fill up an auditorium, and then some, because of the way he lived and loved, I never imagined my life would be this way.

And so, I chuckled, as I had when everyone stood and clapped along to one of his favorite songs, again met with utter disbelief.

These were the words I shared about my precious Chandler on that day:

"For those who don't know me, my name is Alyssa Patterson, I'm Chandler's wife.

"I want to start by thanking everyone for the magnitude of support that has been provided to myself, Chandler's family, and my own over this past week. It's been heartbreakingly beautiful to see all the friends and family surrounding us with prayers, tight hugs, and food.

"I'd also like to express my deepest gratitude to all of the men and women serving across the state's fire departments for their outpouring of love, support, and servants' hearts. Because of you, Chandler is being honored greatly.

"When I began writing this, I knew that there weren't words adequate enough to express my deep sorrow, my love for Chandler, or the love I have for his family and friends that I so proudly call my own.

"A little over three weeks ago, I had begun my final draft of wedding vows, and it is absolutely unbelievable that I'm now eulogizing the man I gave my whole heart to just a few weeks ago. Chandler and I had dreams of traveling to visit our friends in this coming year and doing some projects around our new home, and eventually we planned on starting a family together. It was our greatest dream.

"Being at a total loss for words this week, I've resorted to books to help me piece together my pain.

"A few weeks ago when we got back from our honeymoon, I had started to read one of Chandler's favorite stories as a boy, *Where the Red Fern Grows.*

"The legend from the book goes like this: 'I had heard the old Indian legend about the red fern. How a little Indian boy and girl were lost in a blizzard and had frozen to death. In the spring, when they were found, a beautiful red fern had grown up between their two bodies. The story went on to say that only an angel could plant the seeds of a red fern and that they never died; where one grew, that spot was sacred.'

"When I told him I'd started reading the book, Chandler reminded me that the boy in the book was told by his grandaddy to get something we want, we need to meet God halfway. To step out in faith. But in times like these, God doesn't request the brokenhearted to meet him halfway, or to work hard to find him. Instead, I know our God meets us where we are in the depths of our sorrow. Whether we feel it or not. And I find great comfort in that, and I hope you do too.

"The loss of Chandler is astronomical—this is no secret. Everyone here would agree that he was one of a kind. And as plain as it sounds to say that there is no one like him—it's true.

"Trying to glean something good from the way Chandler lived is so easy, so I want to challenge each of us to be more like he was—vibrant, contagious, and full of light. To live out our days larger than life, to crank the music up maybe a little louder than we should… to put our phones down, to seek fellowship with family and friends, which I'm so thankful we did a lot of this past year. Sometimes even to leave the calendar be for a little while and just be.

"He was the epitome of living life to the fullest, and he filled my days and nights with so much joy and laughter. These last two years, and especially these last three weeks have been the best times of my life because of him.

"Whatever Chandler touched, it turned to gold. He's turned so many hearts to the Lord in the time I had the pleasure of loving him. He was good at pretty much everything, except building gingerbread houses, which I learned last Christmas...

"The evening after the accident, I found myself in the bottom of our shower just staring at the wall asking the question *why* as most of us have. In that moment, this piece of Scripture pressed its way into my heart, and I hope it's something we can all dwell on in the days to come.

John 16:33 says,

"I have told you these things, so that in Me you may have [perfect] peace. In the world you have tribulation and distress and suffering, but be courageous [be confident, be undaunted, be filled with joy]; I have overcome the world." [My conquest is accomplished, My victory abiding.]

"My prayer for myself, and all of you is that the Lord fulfills his promise viciously during the time we all take to grieve the loss of a truly incredible man that I loved with all my heart.

"A part of my life, the most precious and beautiful and joyful parts of my life, has been buried with his. I'm so thankful that in the very least, his life has brought me to love and know all of you. And I am so thankful for all of the moments he and I shared together here on earth. It was only our beginning, but this is not the end. I am certain that Chandler's legacy will live long past all of us and that his life will echo through heaven for eternity."

Shakily I stepped down from the stage and returned to my seat, passing his casket once more. For the remainder of his service, I was so numb, nothing would have surprised me. The roof could have fallen in and I would have been indifferent. The biggest, worst, most horrible thing had already happened to me. But even in the sorrow, I was proud of the words I left for him, and even now, I feel like he heard every single one from his house in heaven.

When Chandler and I started dating, he told me he had always had this premonition that he'd die young, and when he told me, I rolled my eyes and told him to never say that again. But when he spoke those words to me for the first time, in my mind's eye, I saw a packed building and a line wrapped around the building. That is the exact picture of what I saw that day in July as I looked out at the thousands who loved him. I stood in disbelief as my memory and real life were colliding in front of me all at once. And while everyone there loved him so deeply, I knew that no one would feel the emptiness and grief quite the way I did, and still do.

I was his wife. He was my husband. Even now, as I write these words out, the past tense makes me shudder.

There's an old saying that goes "you preach your own funeral by the way you live." Chandler did just that. Only a few weeks prior to his passing, at our rehearsal dinner, he decided to speak very last minute. I told a friend recently that any chance Chandler had to lead a group or call people higher, he took it. And that is exactly what he did on the eve of our wedding.

He took the microphone stand that night, just like I had the day I eulogized him, and welcomed everyone with his rich voice with a drawl that would make any lady's heart melt, and said, "How 'bout that ride in?" and began to brief us on how, when he talked about the people he loved, he would cry. And then he let his heart loose, and I believe he was being obedient to a burden the Lord placed on his heart that night, and I am so grateful he did. His message that night left the perfect goodbye that no one got to hear.

He said, "If you want to be happy, you have to invest in people. We get so caught up chasing money and materialistic and tangible objects, that really do nothing for us. When you die, what are people going to say about you? Are they gonna say, "Man, that guy drove an awesome truck," or, "Man, that guy had nice clothes"? When you're gone, people don't remember those things, people don't care about that. People care about who you are and your heart. If you invest in people, you will always be rich. If you have a full heart, you'll be rich. And you can never have that if you don't pour into other people."

His words that day shocked me. We were getting married the very next day, why was death on his mind? But I knew every word he spoke was true, so I just said, "Preach it, babe" from my chair and let it roll… In the months that passed, his words came to reflect this Scripture so sweetly.

"Do not store up for yourselves [material] treasures on
earth, where moth and rust destroy, and where thieves
break in and steal. But store up for yourselves treasures

in heaven, where neither moth nor rust destroys, and where thieves do not break in and steal; for where your treasure is, there your heart [your wishes, your desires; that on which your life centers] will be also." (Matthew 6:19–21 AMP)

Chandler had a heart of gold and certainly stored up plenty of treasure in heaven by the way he loved me, honored his family, and was a friend to anyone who needed company. I can't wait to see all of the treasures he was storing up in his twenty-seven precious years of life. I am certain it is far more than most can say in a long-lived lifetime. He was my sweetest treasure and carrying on his legacy has brought me great joy, and sharing our story and who he was has given my pain great purpose.

Hellish Days

"Her absence is like the sky, spread over everything. But no, that is not quite accurate. There is one place where her absence comes locally home to me, and it is a place I can't avoid. I mean my own body. It had such a different importance while it was the body of H.'s lover. Now it's like an empty house."

—C.S. Lewis, *A Grief Observed*

$\mathcal{I}$ sat on the couch in our living room, the back door left open with the screen door closed, letting the warm summer breeze blow through the house. I took in a deep breath of fresh air, one of my favorite things in the world. We had honeysuckle vines behind our house, and I hadn't discovered them until my mother-in-law pointed them out after we moved in. It had always been a dream of mine to have a house with honeysuckles in the yard.

I inhaled the scent of the sweet yellow flower, and for the first time, I noticed I was tired. We had held Chandler's celebration of life just a few days prior, and it finally hit me like a Mack Truck. The survival mode had finally worn off, and I was exhausted. The only time I could be coaxed to sleep for thirty minutes or so was in the car. The hum of the engine still soothed me as it had when I was a child.

I looked over at my friends and family who filled the living room that day, and I said, "I think I am ready to take a nap." I hesitated, "But I don't want to be alone."

Looking back, that simple admission was such a symbol of surrender. For the last few weeks, I couldn't sleep by myself. I already felt so alone, why make the hole in my heart bigger by leaving an empty space in the bed beside me? My sister Ava, and one of my best friends Taylor filled the gaps in between and made sure I wasn't alone in bed for a single minute in those early days.

My precious friend Leiah, who had stood beside me on my wedding day, hopped up at my willingness to take a nap that day in July and said, "Let's go." I climbed into my cool soft sheets, and she took a seat at the foot of my bed on the floor. I slept for two hours that afternoon in summer without the help of sleep aid, and I was so grateful to be able to have the bed to myself—but not be left alone.

In those first days and weeks after Chandler's death, I could hardly do anything on my own. My body felt like it had when I came down with an awful case of the flu the first October Chandler and I had been dating. He sent me "Get Well Soon" flowers that arrived on my doorstep on Halloween that year. I was physically weak. I couldn't eat or drink hardly anything, and I was practically left to skin and bone.

On our honeymoon to Cancun we had been pampered with the most delicious food and drinks. When we made our way to the breakfast buffet on our first morning there, we had been pleasantly surprised by the most beautiful arrangement of fruit and fresh tropical juices. Each morning with my breakfast, I ordered a glass of sweet watermelon juice. I also treated myself to many watermelon martinis that had been made with the fresh juice as well. That drink had been a trademark of our trip.

At this point, water still tasted like sulfur, so one day I asked my mom if she could make watermelon juice for me. Just like the watermelon juice I drank each morning while we were on our honeymoon. I think my mother was so excited I was willing to hydrate, that she went to the store or sent someone on her behalf and bought three large watermelons. She cut off the rind, cut it into cubes, and blended it up. It was the only thing that nourished me for a few days, but it instantly transported me back to those perfectly blissful days Chandler and I shared in Cancun.

I took a sip after waking from my nap and closed my eyes as I sat in the sun. I dreamed of our days on the beach that held all the pieces to my perfect life, including my precious husband who loved me so well.

How could so much change so quickly? I wondered as I slowly sipped the sweet pink juice, squinting my eyes up to the sun. *How did this happen to me?*

I needed intercession in every single way in those first days. I couldn't be alone to sleep. I needed to be force-fed or I wouldn't eat. I barely survived on the watermelon juice and saltines. The only task I could do on my own was take a shower... sort of.

One day my mother, out of desperation to see me crack a smile, offered to put her dog in the shower with me. I cried and laughed through my tears as she shoved the dog into my arms. The poor dog wiggled and squirmed until I let her go, and she took off through my house soaking wet covered in suds. It worked—I had laughed. But it didn't last long. The moment my mom went chasing after her, the violent tears came back again.

Some days I would get in the shower and just let the water pour over me as I cried into it, letting it wash every tear away as it came. The shower was one of the places I cried the most, second to our closet where his coats and boots still lived. Being newlyweds, we spent our mornings and evenings talking about our days, in that sweet, safe, and intimate space. Loving one another, laughing together, and brushing our teeth. It was some of my favorite time we got to share together.

In this season of my most painful days, I felt so disconnected and dissociated from my emotions. In the same breath, I could go from feeling totally numb to sobbing at the drop of a hat. I was just trying to survive the pain until Chandler's celebration of life. I relied heavily on sleep aid and was sleeping from 3:00 a.m. until about 4:00 p.m. in the afternoon in those first days. The days and weeks to come were as close as you can get to hell on earth. Unbearable pain, confusion, anger, the groans of mourning, all bottled up in my already tiny body. It was just too much.

In those days when I relied on everyone around me to function, the Holy Spirit, my friends, and family interceded for me in ways I will never forget.

I learned so much about prayer in those vulnerable moments where I couldn't help but be transparent. I imagined myself over and over just collapsing to my knees at the feet of Jesus, washing his feet with my tears of anger and confusion and pain, honoring him still. Somehow.

It was in those moments that I sometimes could only utter three words. But it was in those moments of my little prayers that I felt closest to him.

My magic three-word prayer?

"Help me, Jesus."

I had so much I needed help with and didn't quite know where to begin as it changed daily.

"Help me to seek the good in you, in this mess."

"Help me to feel near to you in this mess."

"Help me to have peace that you have my sweet Chandler in the palm of your hand."

"Help me to not freak out on my family and friends who mean well."

"Help me to endure this gracefully."

"Help me, Jesus."

Thinking back on those simple but honest prayers that were surrounded by so many grief-filled tears, I am thankful the Lord answered them so fully. You see, even then, especially then, and still today, the Lord wants us close to him. He doesn't need an elaborate speech or declaration, although he loves that too. At the end of the day, he just wants his children to bear their heart and soul to him. It was in those "Help me, Jesus" prayers that brought me right to his feet, right where I needed to be.

"Whenever you pray, be sincere and not like the pretenders who love the attention they receive while praying before others in the meetings and on street corners. Believe me, they've already received their reward. But whenever you pray, go into your innermost chamber and be alone with Father God, praying to him in secret. And your Father, who sees all you do, will reward you openly." (Matthew 6:5–6 TPT)

My favorite place to pray, maybe because it was the only place I could be alone, was in our closet. I would lock my bedroom door, and beeline through the bathroom, shutting the closet door behind me. I would step into Chandler's shirts hung up on the rack and let the scent of him dance all around me and fill me up. I would stain them with my tears and wrap my arms around as many t-shirts and jackets as I could and pretend like I was holding him tight just one last time.

In the same sob-filled breath, I would ask God to help me, and then I would ask him "Why?" knowing I would get no answer, and even if I did find an answer or some explanation, I knew nothing, absolutely nothing could justify losing such a man, at such a time, in such a way.

I went to battle in those early days and weeks after losing him and certainly have since, in different ways. I have waged war for my joy. I have fought hard for my peace. But over and over again, I found myself gripping at anything that resembled hope with barely enough strength to hang on. I was exhausted by trying to feel anything but sorrow.

I am so thankful now to know the truth that Jesus was with me in every fit and fight. He sat with me while I yelled at him. He held me close when I felt lonely in such a deep way. He mourned with me when I would weep, not knowing when the tears would end. I cannot tell you how many times I fell to the floor and cried until I couldn't cry anymore, to find a literal pool of tears and spit on the ground beneath me.

Grief is not pretty. But Jesus can handle it because he's endured it. We serve a God who has grieved death. He actually bled, suffered, and died, and in the dying conquered death, taking *true life* back for every one of us.

> "When Jesus saw her sobbing, and the Jews who had come with her also sobbing, He was deeply moved in spirit [to the point of anger at the sorrow caused by death] and was troubled, and said, 'Where have you laid him?' They said, 'Lord, come and see.' Jesus wept."
> (John 11:33–35 AMP)

Jesus gets it. I couldn't get over this part of Scripture after reading it after one of my moments of having it out with all of hell. It says, "He was deeply moved to the point of anger at the sorrow caused by death."

There it is. So honest, bold, and true. We're talking about the perfect Jesus, blameless and whole, who felt the same exact way I did in my own grief. Those words made me feel so much more comfortable in my own moments of anger at the sorrow we had been carrying and will carry in the wake of losing Chandler.

I think I read *A Grief Observed* in the whole of a day or two almost exclusively on our front porch. Sitting in a rocking chair with a glass of ice-cold sweet tea, I read:

"We were promised sufferings. They were part of the program. We were even told, 'Blessed are they that mourn,' and I accept it. I've got nothing that I hadn't bargained for. Of course it is different when the thing happens to oneself, not to others, and in reality, not imagination."[4]

And I remembered the Scripture that had been spoken over and over to me served on baskets of flowers and donned on beautifully designed sympathy cards: "Blessed are those who mourn, for they will be comforted" (Matthew 5:4 NIV).

To love is to expose your heart to the possibility of it being broken. And mine had been broken in the most vile way, how could *I* be called blessed? I learned in those days to come that it wasn't the breaking of my heart and the grief itself that was the blessing, but it was what God could do in that darkness that would bless me greatly. It was in the way he would draw near in the challenging days that followed that would prove his faithfulness.

The Message Translation puts Matthew 5:4 this way:

"You're blessed when you feel you've lost what is most dear to you. Only then can you be embraced by the One most dear to you."

It was barely past those early days of tormenting sorrow when I found myself in an independent study on the book of Lamentations. I was so relieved to find another source in Scripture where brothers and sisters in Christ were grieving so honestly over their own loss. Like me, they too were lost in the throes of sorrow in one breath...

"My soul has been cast far away from peace; I have forgotten happiness. So I say, 'My strength has perished And so has my hope and expectation from the Lord.'" (Lamentations 3:17–18 AMP)

... and found at the peak of worship declaring his goodness in the next.

"But this I call to mind, Therefore I have hope. It is because of the Lord's lovingkindnesses that we are not consumed, Because His [tender] compassions never fail. They are new every morning; Great and beyond measure is Your faithfulness." (Lamentations 3:21–23 AMP)

I found myself constantly somewhere in between in the mourning. Time and time again I would go from mourning to praising back to the mourning once more. My grief was never the same for too long. It was, and is, always changing, pulling me down to the depths of despair and pointing me onward to the eternal in the same breath.

This additional Scripture from our brothers and sisters in Lamentations, the most honest grievers, stuck with me and comforted me greatly in my own efforts to "grieve well." It is honest, transparent, and you can just tell the writer was clinging to the promises of God in their own grief, even still.

"My eyes overflow with streams of tears because of the destruction of the daughter of my people (Jerusalem). My eyes overflow unceasingly, without stopping, until the Lord looks down and sees from heaven. My eyes [see things that] bring pain to my soul because of all the daughters of my city. Without cause my enemies hunted me down like a bird; they silenced me in the pit and placed a stone over me. The waters ran down on my head; I said, 'I am cut off (destroyed)!' I called on Your name, O Lord, out of the lowest pit. You have heard my voice, "Do not hide Your ear from my prayer for relief, From my cry for help." You drew near on the day I called to You; You said, 'Do not fear.' O Lord, You have pleaded my soul's cause [You have guided my way and protected me]; You have rescued and redeemed my life. O Lord, You have seen the wrong [done to me]; judge my case." (Lamentations 3:48–59 AMP)

Emmanuel, God with us. He hears your cries. He knows your grief, intimately. Just like he knows my own. I am ever grateful that in the most hellish days I have held on this earth, the Holy Spirit swept low and pressed in close.

I began the process of changing my last name just a few weeks after Chandler went to heaven. It was an unbearable thing to do. But I believed that he, as my husband, deserved the honor, and that I, as his wife, deserved the privilege even still.

It felt like such a strange choice to make, not the decision itself but the weight around it. To be completely honest, I had gone back and forth on changing my name after the accident even though before, I had fully intended to. It all happened too quickly, my happiest and most blissful days fell far too close to my worst most hellish ones.

But one day I did the hard task of going through a box with items from our wedding day where I found the letter he wrote for me on the morning of June 5. In the letter he penned, *I can't wait for you to take my last name*, and I could hear him saying it still in my dreams. So I did something that should have been blissful and exciting with a heavy heart. Sometime in late summer, I became Mrs. Alyssa Patterson.

I'm so proud to have been his, I'm so proud to have taken his last name as my own. In taking his last name after his death, I inherited a new responsibility as his wife and widow to honor him, and his namesake, and to carry his legacy as long and as far as I possibly can. But this responsibility wouldn't be any different if he was here today.

The mission of a wife and a marriage union is the same, I'm learning, in death and in life. To honor, to build a legacy, and to push the kingdom forward. To balance the dark and the light. I choose to not let the dark shadow of my grief keep the light away. And while there will always be a shadow, it's up to me to decide how much light I let back in. For life still can hold beauty even in the darkness, when you follow the Light.

A Breath of Joy

In a field full of blossoms,
the Father found them so.
Everywhere they needed to be,
not a place they needed to go.
Content in loving the lily pads
and frogs that croaked below.
In a child's eyes, there's no difference
to the one their love should show.

Written spring '18

I n the small, but dear, moments of favor I found with God after Chandler passed away, I learned so fully that he is deeply ingrained in the details of our lives, and he loves it that way.

Chandler and I had just woken up from an afternoon nap a few days into our honeymoon. I rolled over in bed to find him scrolling through Craigslist with "puppy" typed in the search bar.

My tired eyes shot open and I smiled. "A puppy?" He giggled and said I would need someone to keep me company when we returned home and when he returned to his twenty-four hours on, forty-eight hours off shifts at the fire department. We scrolled through the pages of puppies for sale in our area and stopped at a cream and white Shih Tzu. She was just the breed we were looking for, and she was the runt of the litter too!

I stopped him and said, "Look at her! She's perfect!" He proceeded to message the seller, and by the time we were getting ready for our dinner reservation that night, we had FaceTimed with the breeder and the puppy!

We were both beside ourselves with excitement. In a small way, by way of fur-child, we would be starting our family with the addition of this sweet puppy. We would wake to crying in the night. We would have visits at the vet. We would even endure potty training together.

Over dinner that night we talked about names, and we decided a system where I'll name the babies, he'll name the dogs since Chandler was renowned for naming dogs. I can't quite remember how it came to be now, but after quite a few cocktails and throwing out a few options, Chandler and I had landed on the name Hazel.

Later that night we met up with some of our new friends we had met at a poolside bar, Katie and Gunther, for espresso martinis, and we proudly showed them the photos of our new little fur-baby who hadn't even opened her eyes yet! They were so excited with us. We had already sent photos home to the family, announcing our exciting news!

It was all coming together so perfectly. What a beautiful day that was too. We slept in, sat by the pool, napped, puppy shopped, did married people things, and topped the night off cheers-ing drinks with new friends and celebrating something so precious.

I know our marriage wouldn't be like it was that day in Cancun forever. I knew we would fight, he would irritate me, I would annoy him. We were both headstrong people, so it is certain that we had some knock-down-drag-out passionate arguments and make-ups heading for us eventually. But I knew nothing would break us. I knew I would always love him, and he would always love me. We would fight, but we would always fight for each other too.

Chandler never got to meet our sweet Hazel in person. She has been the sweetest gift, and I believe the timing of her was so intended by God.

I have always had the tendency to nurture. Though now it seems like a far-off wish, I have always dreamed of being a momma. Even though I said we were going for the "I'll name the babies and you'll name the dogs" approach, Chandler came up with all the good baby names we had saved for someday too.

My dream has always been to have four boys who all grow up to be bigger than me, and I'd just be their little momma among them all. But when I met and fell in love with Chandler, I wanted nothing more than to see him hold a baby girl of his own, and watch him fall in love with her just like he had fallen in love with me. It was our greatest, most precious dream, and I was so excited to live it out with him. He would have made an incredible dad to our children, and I would have loved the blessing of being able to watch him become a father. It is one of the many things about his passing that I grieve the most.

As nurturing had become a core aspect of my personality in my early twenties, it had been long rooted in a much younger version of me. As a four-year-old, I had requested donations of dog food and dog toys in lieu of gifts to be donated to our local animal shelter for my birthday party. Years later, when I was in middle school, I collected donations for our local animal shelter through a program I created called Christmas for Critters. I still remember how my bedroom overflowed with old blankets, towels, dog food, and cat toys. I still remember the joy I felt delivering the vanload.

So, it makes perfect sense why God would send this sweet puppy, a perfect tiny gift, just a few weeks after Chandler went home to be with Jesus. He was in the details. He had gone before me. And he was preparing more than just one blessing.

The day we were scheduled to pick up Hazel from the breeder, my dad received a call letting us know that another puppy was available.

I had just woken up at my in-laws' house and had snuck into the kitchen to make myself a hot cup of tea. My father-in-law snuck beside me with a large stack of cash, and I had no idea why he was handing me so much money so early in the morning. And then he whispered, "I'm surprising the girls… Hazel's brother became available this morning." For the first time since Chandler passed away, my heart skipped a beat. The kind of leap when it feels like your heart rises out of your tummy. Pure warmth, sweet joy.

As I left that morning, I encouraged my in-laws to meet us later that afternoon to "meet Hazel," and they agreed. We all hugged and said we'd see each other later, and I slipped my father-in-law a wink as I headed out the door, cherishing that sweet secret while I had it. I stepped out the front door and giggled at the sky... *two* puppies? And there that feeling was again: pure warmth, sweet joy.

That afternoon, when my family and I went to meet the breeder to pick up the two puppies, my heart was filled with so much anticipation—the good kind, for a change. I was so grateful to have something else to care for, but my heart broke that Chandler would never be part of the things we had been planning on and dreaming of. But the moment they placed our Hazel in my arms, I knew the tiniest amount of puppy breath was going to do me a whole lotta good.

After a car ride of puppy snuggles, we arrived at our meeting place. Climbing out of the car, I held Hazel in my arms while my sister stayed in the car with Hazel's brother, which my sister-in-law later named Hardy after the country singer Chandler loved so much.

The girls ran up to me, and they cooed at little Hazel, petting her sweet face. We snapped a picture and the surprise was under-way! Up behind them snuck my father-in-law with their little puppy in hand. The girls turned around and realized there was more than one little ball of fur and they both gasped. Tears filled everyone's eyes as we laughed and rejoiced at the sweet, perfect, tiny gifts those little puppies were.

That day was a cornerstone, and even though it was still so early on in our loss and grief, there was still a hint of hope, still a breath of joy, right there in the middle of all of our pain. It has been amazing to see the joy and the pain co-exist so freely in our hearts and homes in our days of grieving.

Long before we knew what would take place on June 26, God was working. As Chandler and I snuggled up in our honeymoon bed, sunburnt and so filled up with love for one another, God was moving. Orchestrating the details of two tiny puppies that would act as a salve to our broken hearts.

One detail that a friend brought to my attention after Chandler's passing was that the name he had chosen for our little puppy, Hazel, means something incredible. *Hazel*, translated in Hebrew, means "God sees."

All this time, since the moment we picked her name over dinner and drinks at our resort in Cancun, God was speaking over me. Over us. He saw us and rejoiced at our marriage. He saw Chandler and embraced him as he welcomed him into his eternal home with Jesus. He saw me when my knees had sunk into the gravel at the lake that day, frozen in shock at my life that had just unraveled, every dream and plan gone. He saw us in the pits of our sorrow, and he saw us when we found a sliver of joy in the tiniest (and fluffiest) little gifts.

We serve a God that is in the details, and a Holy Spirit that meets us in every moment. What a thing to praise! When my sister-in-law and mother-in-law realized that they, too, were now the owners of a sweet little puppy, my mother-in-law exclaimed, "This was the Lord! Was this not the Lord?" And she couldn't have been more right. God orchestrated that blessing, and he was on the move… going far before us, orchestrating many more blessings to come.

My mom used to call them "God winks" when I was small. Just touches of heaven in the everyday, always lifting our tired eyes upward, whispering, calling us, into the eternal.

Matthew 6:30 (TLB) says, "And if God cares so wonderfully for flowers that are here today and gone tomorrow, won't he more surely care for you, O men of little faith?"

I was nineteen or twenty years old and working as a nanny while I was finishing my college degree online with Colorado State University. I found myself many-a-morning with sleepy eyes, tea or coffee in hand, heading to take care of the sweetest family after a long night of studying and paper writing, which had also been fueled by more tea and coffee. One morning as I drove to my nannying job, I was struck by a beautiful pasture in the most precious valley. It was mid-summer, and the early morning sun was pushing up through the storm clouds that had already arrived. I pulled over to write this sweet story that today, makes me see just how close heaven was to my heart even then, and how much nearer it would draw to me in the years to come.

I turned down the radio and thought I had never seen a stormy sky resemble heaven so much. Being met with such a strong reality at only six in the morning will make a tired person think more than they'd typically like to. But instead of running from the idea of heaven being right in front of me, tangible through the drops of rain,

I wrestled with it. Why do the clouds always look like longing minutes before it pours?

I thought on the question while my exhausted eyes squinted out the window.

Being a reasoner, I welcomed in thoughts on the rules of condensation and the water cycle. But in this moment, my Father in heaven wanted me to think on something more abstract. I believe that God places parallels like these all over his creation for us to learn more of his heart, but most of the time, the answers he desires us to find aren't buried in textbook and reason. His answers—the ones much farther from reason and in a place much more confusing, the heart—are only there if we choose to look for them.

So, on this particular day, I reminisced with the heavy clouds above, and discovered all my longings were the same—incomplete entirely, until I one day stand beside my Father in heaven. My longing to finish school, my longing to have lasting friendships, my desire to find my life partner. All, even when met with completion, will leave me unsatisfied unless I am walking with my Father.

"Meet me near the moon, up among the stars. Chase me and you'll find me." This is our Father's plea. "Join me?" he whispers gently through stormy skies, patiently waiting for us to turn our

Tired.

Eyes.

Up.

All my desires were the same even then, even now. Everything utterly pointless without the hope of heaven, and incomplete without the one who makes it so.

Heaven comes close in the ordinary and is even closer in the miserable days of grief if we allow it to. Our God delights in bringing the things of heaven into the details of our lives, even in something as seemingly insignificant as the name of a puppy, or the perfect provision of making a second one available for the comfort of a grieving family.

Psalm 37:23 (NLT) says this, "The Lord directs the steps of the godly. He delights in every detail of their lives."

By way of a few sweet, small puppies, the Lord's favor and his delighting in the details was made tangible in puppy love, which was such a precious gift in such a terrible time. To find even a small remnant of healing, a piece of his creation began to stir within us the smallest bit of joy again. A promise that he sees us in our pain and a nod that the Lord cares about providing us with bursts of joy and laughter, even in the sorrow. Especially so.

The Four Loves

Into the eyes of daisies,
another golden thing.
One gentler than a
wildfire,
but not a pinch weaker.
There is strength in
her silence and ancient
myths in her movement.
Just one touch gives
beautiful sight to the fullness of
life.
And as the snow glitters,
far different from when
the sun burned in June,
a single smile from her
takes you right back—
into the eyes of daisies.

Written spring '18

When Chandler and I met, and even up until the time we got married, he had two cars. A red Toyota Tacoma he affectionately called Ruby, and a Toyota Corolla he called Cora. I was a sucker for a good pickup truck, and when I saw him climb out of the Tacoma in his baby blue polo that matched his eyes the night of our first date, I knew I was done for! But Cora... she was his favorite. The first time I got in it, I was stunned, and not in the best of ways... The fabric ceiling had been torn to shreds, "by cats," he said. I laughed.

He looked at me and said, "No, I am serious, I bought this car from an old lady, and she let her cats live in here." He cleaned her up as best as he could, and she quickly became his favorite car. To him, she was indestructible. He "rode that thing all across the state, even crossing state lines," he told me one day proudly. "She isn't ever gonna stop running," he said.

On June 12 when we returned home from our honeymoon, we landed at the airport and took the shuttle back to the hotel we stayed at the night before we left, and where he had parked his precious Cora. We were so tired from traveling and were so ready to just be home and settle into our new life together, but God had other plans besides a seamless trip home.

We threw our luggage into the back seat and climbed in the car. Chandler turned the key, the engine revved, once, twice, and then cut off. We gave each other one of those side-eye glances that says "oh no" without speaking a word. He turned the key again, and the engine revved, once, twice, and then cut off again. He took a deep breath, doing his best to hold his composure. Meanwhile, I was doing my best not to panic, assuming the worst-case scenario: we'd just been stranded in Atlanta and were going to have to call our mom and dad to come to *pick us up from our honeymoon*!

He popped open the hood of the car and jiggled some parts on the battery line that had rusted and just didn't want to stay where they needed to. He told me to turn the key while he tried to put the things in their place. I leaned over and turned the key, the engine revved, once, twice, and then she held on.

Our next stop was food—and fast. We were on our way to getting "hangry," and it was coming up even quicker with the car troubles behind us. We swung through a Wendy's for some spicy nuggets and fries, and we were on our way to the interstate. We were smooth sailing until we reached I-85. If you know Atlanta at all, you know I-85 to be a jungle of cars, pickups, and semi-trucks all being handled by the state's most terrible drivers. We were so ready to be back to the northeast Georgia suburbs...

The car stalled two more times on I-85. And both times, he was able to get us over two or three lanes of traffic just as all of the dials on the dash went down, AC cut, and radio died. He jumped out of the car again, popped the hood, and jiggled the parts around while I cranked the key. It's laughable now, but after a long wedding week, and a honeymoon's worth of partying in us, we were so ready to be in our home together getting into our own rhythm. We needed to get a load of laundry under way, and we both were in desperate need of a hot shower.

Car trouble and all, my sweet groom was determined to carry me over the threshold, and Cora was going to get us there one way or another...

When we finally made it back to our sweet home, after a few more interludes of pulling the car over and cranking the key, before he let me walk through the front door, he stopped me and said, "Wait! You can't come in until I carry you over the threshold!" He paused to situate his phone up against a chair and videoed the whole thing. His robust voice exclaimed, "The first time we step through our home as a married couple! Be prepared!" I laughed as he scooped me up in his sailor arms (think Popeye). As he swung me through the front door he said, "We did it!" as he kissed me and spun me around. We were one. We were home. And he was all mine.

This sweet memory is one that makes me giggle often now, and I wish we could laugh about it together. I wish I could hear him tell the story. He was so good at telling stories. And yet, here I am telling ours.

During the first few weeks after Chandler passed away, our home was constantly filled with the people we loved most. I think subconsciously I was nervous that people constantly being in our home during such an overwhelming and vulnerable time would burden me, but it honestly brought me so much comfort and encouragement in those early days. Some of my sweetest memories in those days was getting to drink wine with my girlfriends and talk about the details of our honeymoon through tear-filled laughter, and to sit around with Chandler's best friends, and listen to them exchange stories from their college years, and even a few tales from his bachelor trip.

It was so strange to have a house that was so full, while everyone inside it was totally emptied. There wasn't a thing that could fill us up, and the commonality of that brokenness pulled us together even tighter than we had already been.

Something strangely painful, something I didn't expect to be, was that many of our friends and family were seeing our new house for the first time, and instead of giving the grand tour of everything we'd worked, dreamed, and prayed for *together*, I was giving it alone. It was so bizarre. I think at times I just pretended he was showing off the garage to his buddies—proudly displaying his new toolbox that had been given to us as a wedding present from my dad.

While I had been in fear of feeling overwhelmed by the company, as days turned into weeks and people left one by one, or more often times two by two, my heart ached even more. I didn't want to be alone. I didn't want to feel his absence more than I had already. But with every couple that walked out of our front door and every car that left our driveway, his absence got bigger and bigger and bigger.

But as the people left, I learned in a painful way that I couldn't grieve the same with company, as I could in solitude. I did grieve with people around, and community has served such a huge purpose in my healing, but there are some things you can only accomplish with solace in the presence of the Lord.

Once things settled, I enjoyed the quiet, as it gave me the necessary time and space to get really honest with my grief. It was in those days that I had to sit in the unbearable silence of our home, shower alone, and sleep alone, to allow the reality of my new life to really settle into the cracks of my broken heart. To say it was painful would be an understatement. I've never lost a limb, but when you do, they speak of phantom pain, which is pain in the place where that limb used to be even though it has since been removed. I had phantom pain for Chandler. I felt him in the night. I had dream after dream that he was alive. I often still do. I had become so used to having him by my side at all times, hearing his voice, his laugh. I got used to the way his toes never stopped moving when we'd lie on the couch to watch a movie. All the little things I loved most about him became a beautiful habit, and in the absence of it all, I had lost what had become a huge piece of myself.

The Lord drew near to me in those days, when I couldn't get close enough to the floor or bury myself deep enough in his shirts that hung in our closet. It was in the quiet when the house emptied that my heart did too, even more than before, and I felt the Lord press in even closer.

And even so, there were some days, granted they were far and few between, that I didn't feel a thing. There were some days I felt completely isolated from God. There were other days when I could only feel the sting of the quiet and the absence of my husband. But some days it was just as healing and productive to just feel the absence, acknowledge how much it hurt, and accept my new reality.

Even in the acknowledgment, especially so, I knew the Lord was near. He hung in the balance of every brokenhearted moment with me. Present as he's ever been in my life. It was a precious gift in my darkest days to feel my Father carrying me through.

The Psalms illustrate this so well—the battle between feeling ever isolated from God, and in a moment, as swift as a whisper, his spirit can fill the room. Psalm 34:18 (ESV) says this, "The Lord is near to the brokenhearted and saves the crushed in spirit."

The Passion Translation puts this same Scripture so beautifully: "The Lord is close to all whose hearts are crushed by pain, and he is always ready to restore the repentant one."

It is only in the greatest of pain that we can recognize our great need for a great God. It is only in our darkest moments when we're completely emptied of ourselves that his spirit is able to fill a room. My relationship with the Lord wouldn't have the same level of intimacy as it would have without the pain that I endured in losing Chandler. I would never know the battle between feeling isolated from God, and feeling his spirit fill the room, mending the cracks of my broken heart.

Jesus said in Matthew 17: 20 (TPT), "I promise you, if you have faith inside of you no bigger than the size of a small mustard seed, you can say to this mountain, 'Move away from here and go over there,' and you will see it move! There is nothing you couldn't do!"

I had big faith in those early days, believe it or not. I think in some ways the shock kept me steadfast. But days, weeks, and even months later when the reality of his death became well known, I found myself with an attitude of impossibility. You could say that most days, even a mustard seed was a generous resemblance of my faith. But even when it was a fraction of such, I knew God was still good, and still trustworthy. Even when I couldn't understand

and unravel my own belief (or unbelief for that matter), in those truths I leaned in hard and kept pressing on.

I cried in my closet, in the shower, on the hardwood of my kitchen floor, and I would let heaven and hell have it. They heard the best and worst of me in those days, and sometimes still do. I think one of the most awful realizations in a loss like this is that while the pain subsides for longer periods of time, in between it is always there, like a blister on your foot from high heels or ballet slippers. The immediate pain is unbearable. You treat it with something that burns and is somehow supposed to help, and for some time it does, but that place is always sensitive and one day the blister will break open again, and you can hardly help walking without looking a little bit gimpy.

The tears I have shed for losing Chandler far too soon will always be a part of me, for however long I am left on this earth. I will carry the grief just as I carry the gratitude. I have come to acknowledge that the pain will surprise me in the shadows of a birthday, or on a happy holiday, or maybe just on a regular day in June. It will all flood back as it did in the beginning, and I will once again, quite gladly, have it out with heaven and hell, and be glad to know that a mustard seed is all I need on those most difficult days. And thank goodness that it is so.

After a few weeks in the quiet, I rolled my office chair away from the desk, pushed myself up out of the seat, and went downstairs to the garage. We didn't have a basement in the house so I told Chandler when we moved in that the garage could be his "man cave." Trump garb, a firefighter flag, and any kind of animal that could be mounted covered the walls. I breathed in the feeling of him and hopped into the front seat of his Tacoma, the one he had climbed out of on our first date. In the console of his truck, just beneath his radio, was where he kept the random love letters I would leave once in a while for him to find early that next morning when he would leave for work. I pulled them out, set them in my lap, and ran my hands over the steering wheel, imagining his hands in mine.

The truck was untouched from the last time he had driven it. Among the things I found was a copy of *The Four Loves* I had given him as a gift. I admit now that it was maybe more of a homework assignment in our early dating days than a present, but nonetheless, I am glad he at least began to read it. He used another love note I had written him as a bookmark. I also found his red tobacco pipe, which matched the bright color of his Tacoma. I gathered my treasures—the book, the notes, and the pipe—and climbed out of the front seat and hopped up on the tailgate. The garage door was open, and the warm summer wind kissed my skin like he should have been able to in that moment.

I breathed in the smells of summer, fresh-cut grass, and the shreds of tobacco that were leftover in his pipe. I read through my letters to him, feeling every bit of love I had for him when I had penned each letter. Our love grew deeper with every page I wrote.

I flipped through my highlighted copy of *The Four Loves* that he never finished reading and stopped on a page marked up with green and blue highlighters. This is what I highlighted all those years ago:

"To love at all is to be vulnerable. Love anything and your heart will be wrung and possibly broken. If you want to make sure of keeping it intact you must give it to no one, not even an animal. Wrap it carefully round with hobbies and little luxuries; avoid all entanglements. Lock it up safe in the casket or coffin of your selfishness. But in that casket, safe, dark, motionless, airless, it will change. It will not be broken; it will become unbreakable, impenetrable, irredeemable. To love is to be vulnerable."[5]

I had highlighted those words, romanticizing them in my mind long before I came to know and deeply love my precious Chandler. I loved him more fully than I ever knew I was capable of, and my heart broke into a billion and one pieces the day he went to heaven. The Lord has been oh so tender and kind to patch up my heart that had been so abruptly broken.

Safely and gently, he is restoring me, one piece at a time.

The Chick Inn

She's on the move. This much is sure.
Not knowing where she'll go, shall not deter.
Looking forward she goes, just the wind, the Creator & her.

Written fall '18

$\mathcal{I}$ boxed up all of Chandler's clothes a few weeks before I was set to close on the sale of our home we had purchased together just a few months prior. That night, as I took down button-downs and ball caps, throwing each piece into a box, I felt pieces of me being boxed up too. I spent a few tear-filled hours that night, shoving so much life into the moving boxes we had hardly unpacked. I couldn't bear to look at his things hanging there with the knowledge that he would never come home and put on those old Tony Lamas ever again.

Once everything had been packed up around 10:00 p.m., a distinct heaviness and darkness came over our home that I can't quite describe, but I knew the moment I taped the last box shut that I couldn't stay.

Immediately, through sobs of heavy grief, I grabbed my toothbrush, threw some random clothes in a bag, and picked up little Hazel who was a few months old and a few pounds heavy at the time. I walked through each room of the house, starting in our closet, where his clothes had been removed, an acknowledgment that he would never be coming back to me this side of heaven. I sat on the floor and cried and prayed in the closet one last time, where I had cried many tears and prayed many prayers in the few weeks before. I bid our bathroom goodbye where we had brushed our teeth and showered together in the mornings and evenings. I walked through our bedroom where love had been made, but not nearly enough. I closed the door behind me, with my duffle bag and puppy dog in hand.

I walked through our guest bedroom where we had hoped to host our friends and family for many nights. I crossed the hall to my office. This was the room I spent the most time saying goodbye to. This was the room that was meant to one day become a nursery. I sat in the floor once more and looked out the front window at the quiet street below. I closed my eyes and listened closely. I could hear the children playing in the summer night just down the road and grieved for a few horrid moments for our children that would never be. I paced in that room for a minute or two, making sure things were somewhat in order, knowing I wouldn't be coming back, knowing I was bidding so much more than a bedroom goodbye.

Much more than a home, I was saying goodbye to each and every one of our precious dreams.

I started down the stairs with all the random things I had packed so quickly, all the bags nearly falling out of my arms. I checked the book nook under the stairs one last time for any books that hadn't been boxed up yet. It had been cleared. Each shelf as empty as my heart.

The kitchen and living room had been emptied too. The whole house was barren, and so was I.

I walked out the front door he had carried me through when we returned home from our honeymoon just a few weeks before. I closed my eyes and imagined that sweet moment before locking the door behind me one last time. I loaded up my car with tears stinging my eyes, knowing I had to gather myself enough to drive to my parents' house.

When I walked in the front door and dropped my bags down, little Hazel running under my feet following me in, I looked at my parents and said with heavy mournful tears, "I can't go back." They came to me and held me as I cried in their arms knowing this was just one more step into the reality of Chandler's passing, and one more step forward into everything new the Lord was already doing.

"This house has chickens!" my dad said from the kitchen table. My stomach sank, burning, remembering the dreams Chandler and I had of one day buying some land, building a home, and getting chickens of our very own. The dreams we once shared now belonged to only me.

I shrugged my shoulders. "Let's go see it," I said somewhat begrudgingly. The open house was on an overcast Sunday afternoon. I stepped into the front door, and the sweet realtor hosting the home said, "Isn't it so cute?" I smiled at her softly and didn't say a word. I ran through the house in a total of five minutes, but likely less, and as I think back on it now, I am not even sure I took a look at the chicken coop. I hardly looked around before I found myself with my head in my hands on the front porch of my home-to-be. I didn't want to leave behind the life I had, but I knew I couldn't stay there. The steps forward, not moving on from loss, but moving forward with the grief and gratitude heavy packed on your back at the same time is one of the most painful and exhausting things I think a person can experience.

We made an offer on the home, and it was accepted the very next day. I was grateful—and grieving still. I was in pain, but thankful the burden of finding a new place to live had been lifted. I was joyful that I knew I could have our little chicken dream at the very least. Living out a dream we had shared together would bless me greatly in the days of healing. In a small way, I feel that it lets a piece of us live on in my life with me. I am so thankful for the Lord's provision and favor in those days of transition. He took care of me then. He is taking care of me still.

I woke up a few weeks later in my bedroom at my parents' house, and in many ways, I felt as if I had been thrown back in time three or four years. I was living with them once again after the beautiful crescendo of falling in love with Chandler, planning our wedding and our life together, and becoming his wife. Every bit of it crumbled on top of me. As my eyes opened that morning and tears stung my eyes once more at the prospect of another day without him, my early morning brain recalled a dream I had had the night before.

The dream opened with my mother and mother-in-law together, teary-eyed cooing at a baby boy with dark hair like mine and blue eyes like Chandler's. We sat together with tears of grief and gratitude, celebrating the blessings all while mourning the loss. In a moment, chaos broke. Chandler was alive, but not in the way we were. I scrambled my things together, and the next thing I knew I was running up a long winding driveway. It was snowing, I was laughing and singing Christmas carols. I arrived home, and the season changed to spring. Everything was green and lush and alive just like it was so on our wedding day in June. I looked into a tree line and found Chandler in the middle of the woods, which is just where he liked to be best. I tried to run to him, but he just got farther from me. I couldn't move. I called out to him, and he didn't answer. He just looked at me, and I knew he saw me. He smiled.

Seasons changed once more. It was early fall, just as the leaves started to change color on the trees. I left the tree line and turned toward the house, walking through its front door. I walked up the stairs into a bedroom with a slanted wall from the way the roof was laid, with a drawn window beside it, and in the bedroom, Hazel was curled up on the floor. A man stood with his back to me holding the baby from the beginning of my dream, and as the newborn cried, I asked if he wanted me to take him, and he said, "I've got it." And I could hear the smile in his voice when he said it. He wore a backward hat and a Carhart yellow shirt. He felt familiar but nothing was the same.

God was doing a new thing.

About three weeks after I had that dream, we road up the long winding driveway to my new home for the final walkthrough. I walked through the living room to the kitchen and got a better look at the master bath this time around. I walked up the stairs, turned left, and walked into a bedroom with a slanted wall from the way the roof was laid, with a window drawn beside it. I stopped dead in my tracks, took a shuddering breath trying to hold back the tears as I reconciled the dream that I had forgotten I'd had.

After I settled into the house, I found myself drawn to a tree line on the east side of our property, the place where the sun rises each and every morning. I never took time to look at it before moving in, but I felt the pull to admire it closely on this day. As I was walking the dog, I found myself lost in it, and again, had to hold back the tears as I reconciled the dream I had forgotten with the reality that was mine. I had seen Chandler there, in the east, the place where the sun rises every morning, and I knew that was where he would meet me in every season.

After the accident, I found myself reading through old text messages Chandler had sent me. One day I stumbled upon one message, in particular, a dream he'd had that aligned so perfectly with my own. His text read:

"I was hunting. The setting was in the most beautiful place ever. The forest was lush green, the water blue, butterflies flying around everywhere. I was stalking around in the woods and then I saw movement through the trees. I could see that it was a beautiful woman dancing in an all-white dress. You had flower lace around the crown of your head too. You looked like an angel. Although I knew that it was you in my dream, in my heart it felt like the first time I had seen you. I slowly approached you in awe of your every move. This is no lie. I came within about ten yards of you, and we made eye contact. I hit my knees, dropped my head, and started crying. You kneeled down, grabbed my face, one hand on each cheek. You lifted my head and said, 'I've been waiting for you, Chan Patterson.' I instantly woke up, and my heart was pounding out of my chest. It was one of the most beautiful, meaningful, and surreal dreams I've ever experienced.

"I think the message God was sending me is that even in that moment, in the dream, it may have seemed like your beauty was at its peak. A beautiful dress, a beautiful setting, a beautiful woman dancing. You were doing what makes your soul happy. Everything seemed to be perfect and like it could not be topped. But, when you looked at me, I was reminded that no matter what, I would love you more every day because true love is always growing. Our love will have extreme highs where in our hearts, we will both be dancing in a field of daisies. Our love will have lows, where we may feel like our love is placed in a murky swamp. Regardless, true love is a covenant. This dream spoke to me in that I have been blessed with something extremely special. Fight for it, love it, and secure it. It won't be easy, but worth it."

I have cried many tears over this text he sent me just a few months after we had met. Since he died, it was like our dreams collided. He had always been waiting for me there, in the woods.

To me, those dreams signified so much. An abundance of blessings in the fulfillment of the same dreams he and I had shared and cherished, in a new way. It also left me with peace that Chandler would always be with me, safeguarding me from heaven. He would be in my midst always, and heaven too would be the same. Anytime I need to find him, I need only to seek the woods. In the Creator's creation, I could find Chandler rolling through the breeze with the Holy Spirit beside him.

In more grief than I could handle, God had gone before me. He swung low and spoke to my broken heart while I rested in sleep and went ahead of me to prepare the blessing. And even now when it feels impossible, I know he goes before me still. Even when I had barely a mustard seed of faith, and even too much grief to care, God was in the details, preparing the blessings to come.

God is able when we aren't able. God is good when our life is anything but. In Paul's letter to the church at Corinth, he wrote, "And God is able to make all grace [every favor and earthly blessing] come in abundance to you, so that you may always [under all circumstances, regardless of the need] have complete sufficiency in everything [being completely self-sufficient in Him], and have an abundance for every good work and act of charity" (2 Corinthians 9:8 AMP).

God is able. He makes all grace come in abundance to you. So, despite your circumstances, you will be complete *in him*.

Even though I couldn't have my husband back, and I can never have the same exact beautiful life he and I would have shared together, I can't help but notice the way my Father in heaven has provided a way in the desert before me, providing for me just like my earthly father and father-in-law have.

My dad gave Chandler my hand in marriage on that beautiful day in June. He trusted Chandler immensely to love and protect me for the rest of our days. When Chandler passed away, so many came alongside me to love me and shepherd me through a season of total devastation. My father stepped back into his role as my primary protector to safeguard me in the ways only a loving father or husband could, and my Father in heaven filled the gaps in between. He worked miracle after miracle to make me a home that held some of Chandler's and my sweet dreams, not making me to live in the shadow of those dreams alone, but to take them up as my own and to live them out for the two of us.

I like to joke that the Lord blessed me in abundance with this new home and all the animals the way he did Job. Abundant blessings, especially by way of livestock. Just two months before,

I had owned zero animals, and after Chandler passed away, our family gained two new puppies and six spry chickens.

"The Lord restored the fortunes of Job when he prayed for his friends, and the Lord gave Job twice as much as he had before. Then all his brothers and sisters and all who had known him before came to him, and they ate bread with him in his house; and they consoled him and comforted him over all the [distressing] adversities that the Lord had brought on him. And each one gave him a piece of money, and each a ring of gold. And the Lord blessed the latter days of Job more than his beginning; for he had 14,000 sheep, 6,000 camels, 1,000 yoke of oxen, and 1,000 female donkeys." (Job 42:10–12 AMP)

The miracle I find in this text is that the Lord restored Job's fortune while he spent his time in prayer *for his friends*, and the Lord doubled his blessing in doing so. Job faced the death of ten of his children, the death of all of his servants and livestock as well as battling his own illness and more. Yet, he was somehow still focused outside of himself. Talk about a selfless soul.

He grieved greatly and sat in silence with his closest friends for days because sometimes saying nothing and just spending time is a more deeply healing remedy than solutions or words. It was when Job turned from his own suffering and faced heaven, bringing the names of his friends and family to the throne room of God that his blessings were revealed abundantly.

Chandler will never be replaced. He couldn't be. No one who passes away should be—or can. But I know, claim, and believe greatly that God is able to bless us anyway. God doesn't stop being good, or righteous, or just when we can't understand. He is still good. He is still sovereign. He is still advocating for us even in our anger, sorrow, and unbelief.

He is with you. He will bless you. Eternity by his side is the ultimate gift.

Never Alone

Good November morning,
among the breeze I hear your calling.
Whispering to my tender soul,
"You're free, just fall, let go."

Written fall '18

I cried the whole time I drove. It was one of the first times I had the luxury of about forty-five minutes of assured time alone since Chandler had passed. I talked to Jesus through tears the whole drive to that first counseling session. As I pulled my car into a parking spot, I put the car in park and flipped down my sun visor and slid open the mirror to check myself before heading in. I was so brokenhearted for the girl I saw looking back at me. Her eyes puffy, her hair braided because it hadn't been brushed or washed in days. I hadn't put makeup on in weeks, and today was no different. As I looked upon myself, I saw that the beautiful bride who had just come to life inside of me had died too. She was weary, tired, hungry for the things of heaven, and ready to wrangle this mess called grief.

I took a deep breath and closed my eyes, picturing Chandler side by side with Jesus far off in some eternal mountain range. I stepped out of my car and walked toward the front of the counselor's office, and as my hand met the door handle, all I could think was "I shouldn't be here." In fact, when I was ushered to my counselor's office that was one of the very first things that I said to him, "I shouldn't be here." I cried between words. He looked at me with such empathy, a face I had come to know well in those days. The facial expression where the eyebrows furrow inward and the smile turns down to one side.

He answered me in agreeance. "No, you shouldn't be. You were his wife for three weeks. You shouldn't be here." I was relieved that we were on the same page. Thankful that he agreed with me. He didn't want to fix what had happened to me, or even fix how I was reacting to what had happened to me, but to guide me through it, continually pointing me to the promises of Christ, ushering me gently to the hope of eternity.

So, we started from the beginning. I told him the long list of things I loved most about Chandler, like his eagerness to do his best at anything he tried his hand in, or his uncanny ability to befriend any stranger. I told him how Chandler told me he was going to marry me on our very first date, and we laughed together at what integrity and honesty his statement had held. I was, and forever will be, so grateful that his promise was fulfilled. In that moment of gratitude, I stayed there and expressed to my counselor how grateful I was to have loved him and to have been loved by him. I was so grateful he chose me to be his wife and that I was the one who got to be his bride. I told him that knowing what I knew now, I would have married him all over again. And again, and again, if I could. He was my greatest treasure, and I wouldn't have traded him for the world.

When I left the office, the sun was peering through the clouds, and I began to feel just a little bit lighter. I felt that, even though there was a long and trying road before me, I could choose hope, knowing that I was on the brink of eternity with every raindrop and falling leaf in November. Heaven was and would be in my midst forevermore.

In the days before me, I had to wrangle and wrestle my grief into being my friend, which is a nice way to put it… More honestly, I went to war with it. I hated it. I hated that life had brought me here, to such deep sorrow at such a young age. I didn't want to be a widow. I didn't want to grow bitter. I didn't want to live my life alone. I didn't want to live my life without Chandler. It's why I married him after all.

Through my endless hours of inner dialogue, out-loud prayers up to heaven, and sometimes my necessary downward declarations to hell that Satan doesn't win, I shed layer by layer of pain through honest worship. And in time, I learned to welcome my grief like an old friend without having to wrestle it to the ground first. I learned to welcome the grief in, to come and stay awhile, and take a grateful walk with me down my most precious memory lane, ushering it to leave when it was time to go.

But be assured, I can promise you I don't always have that friendly relationship with my grief. I still fight with it often and surely will for years to come. But it will never leave me. It will merely change. And I hope as the years pass by, I can continue to welcome my grief like a friend on the days that it wells up inside me.

Community and wise counsel have ushered me gently and lovingly to this truth and this hope. Now I can treat my grief like a friend, and when I find myself sending praise up to heaven, I find myself just a little more healed, or lighter in the least.

I am so grateful for the people who leaned in and came around me and my family in the wake of Chandler's death. I don't know how people make it through a loss so huge without community and wise counsel that continually encourages us to turn our weary eyes up to the hope of heaven on the days that the sorrow is too great to see beyond our circumstances.

In Chandler's speech at our rehearsal dinner on the eve of our wedding day, he encouraged us all to "invest in people," and because he had done that so well in his beautiful twenty-seven years of life, he left me with a wonderful crowd of friends, blood relatives that became my very own in our marriage, and a very special Fire Family to come alongside me in his passing. The support I received from my community and family, and am still receiving daily, has been an essential cornerstone alongside my faith, and counseling, that has immensely impacted my grieving process.

Just as Chandler said in his speech, the book of Genesis reminds us of the same: "Now the Lord God said, 'It is not good (beneficial) for the man to be alone'" (Genesis 2:18 AMP).

Think about it this way: it wasn't good for man to be alone when the conditions of the world were totally perfect. So, of course in a time of grief, just like Job had, we need company. We were made for community.

The sweetest moments with my friends and family in those early days of grief, so tender and painful, were simply a long hug and an "I love you," sometimes not a word more needing to be said, because those three words said everything we needed to know.

To accept wise counsel in grief and to accept loving community in grief are both choices—and difficult ones at that. Growing up, and still today, my dad has always said that "life is about choices," and it is ever true. We can't control everything that happens to us. If we could, I wouldn't be writing this book. I am sure of that. However, we do have the choice of how we react to the things that do happen to us.

I felt greatly burdened after Chandler's death that it became my responsibility, and strange honor, to memorialize his life and love for me in any way that I could. I wanted to stretch his voice and his story as far and wide as possible. And so, I made a choice to lean into God in a time where, to some, it made quite little sense to. Why get closer to a God who "let this happen"? To you, I say, because this battle we're fighting is bigger than today and any world war that could be waged, and the good news is that it was finished before my worst day had even begun. My husband went to his eternal home, and the fact that death did not take him prisoner is a gift straight from the cross. I trust *that* God. The God who made a way. The God who took up the whole weight of eternal death upon himself so that we'd never die and that we would spend eternity in his presence instead.

So I gathered my first fruits, which happened to be a single mustard seed of faith, and in my confusion and deep sorrow, I leaned into the Lord knowing that the only way I would see to the other side of this was if I was abiding in him, letting his word and my worship saturate my broken heart in the salve that is salvation and the medicine that is mercy.

"So you must remain in life-union with me, for I remain in life-union with you. For as a branch severed from the vine will not bear fruit, so your life will be fruitless unless you live your life intimately joined to mine." (John 15:4 TPT)

I boarded the flight to Phoenix at around six o'clock in the morning. I felt so much anticipation for the weekend ahead of me, and I was so ready to be filled up with fellowship from other women who would understand my pain in a way no one else could.

I was, in the strangest way, excited. Butterflies met me as the plane touched down in a city I had never been to. I wandered through the airport terminals down to baggage claim, looking for a group of women I had never met before. First Brie, next Christy, then Gracie. We exchanged hugs and did our best to remember names, asking politely about each other's flights, as the elephant in the room was filling up the terminal. We were all meeting for the same reason as the next girl. Our husbands had died, and each of them were called American heroes. Whether they were marked by a military or first responder seal, we had all loved and married some of the world's bravest and boldest men, and we had lost them too.

This retreat was hosted by a beautiful ministry called Never Alone Widows, which is put on by some of the most incredible, Christlike women I have ever known. It was so humbling to sit at their feet and listen to their own testimonies of loss and finding love again, reclaiming the joy that had been stolen from them, just like it had been from me.

That weekend was filled with laughter and tears, and bonds were formed like nothing else I have ever experienced.

Like I usually do, I sought out quite a few moments of solitude on that trip. One morning I woke a few minutes earlier than the rest to sit on the patio with my Bible splayed open, and as the hot Phoenix sun rose over the mountains and cactus, I just knew I was going to be okay. I could feel Chandler and Jesus close in that moment in the warmth of the sun brushing my skin, and I knew though I would be apart from them both until I returned to my eternal home, they would be with me always.

"Her!"

The way he exclaimed it from across the river made me blush.
In an instant I knew I was loved, I knew I was worth crossing every river for.
For my God leaves the ninety-nine."

Written about my Jesus, sometime in 2018

A few months after attending my retreat with Never Alone Widows, I was reunited with many of the women I met that weekend in November. As I sat at the first ever Never Alone Widows Conference in Atlanta, Georgia, my eyes were truly opened to the fact that the same beautiful work the Lord was doing in my life, he was doing in the lives of many. He was making a way for hundreds of women, just like me.

As the room filled with two hundred and fifty other widows who knew the pain I had endured all too well, I didn't see widows dressed in mourning clothes, with the exception of a few that were especially sorrowful on the first night. They were heavy-laden with the burning tears of grief. But by the afternoon on the next day, in just a twenty-four-hour time span, the Lord had revealed the sweetest sight to my heart. It wasn't a room full of mourning clothes that I saw, but a room full of beautiful brides dressed in white—veils and all.

I imagined them each, as they left with faces refreshed and hearts filled with the Holy Sprit, walking out the doors into the loving arms of their heavenly husband, Jesus. Bouquet in hand, running toward the cross.

I will always be Chandler's bride, and that is my favorite gift. But I've always been the bride of Christ first and foremost. Even in my singleness, even in my widowhood. I am still a bride, and so are you. Cherished, pursued, and wildly loved.

My heavenly husband, Jesus, provides for me, chases after me, and will always be my kinsman redeemer.

> "I saw the Holy City, the New Jerusalem, descending out
> of the heavenly realm from the presence of God, like a
> pleasing bride that had been prepared for her husband,
> adorned for her wedding. And I heard a thunderous
> voice from the throne, saying: 'Look! God's tabernacle is
> with human beings. And from now on he will tabernacle
> with them as their God. Now God himself will have his
> home with them—"God-with-them" will be their God!'"
> (Revelation 21:2-3 TPT)

Wait Expectantly, Dear Heart

I spent my evenings
staring up at the stars
in wonder of everything
that you are.
I spent my mornings
searching for you, moon,
in awe of how you'd
proven faithful so soon.
And the time in between,
well those moments meant
everything.
It's the time that the moon,
the stars, and each creation
in the sky came together
to beautifully reflect that
The Son:
He's still alive.

Written fall '18

$\mathcal{H}$ ope, just like love, at some point ceases to be a feeling and begins to be a choice, especially when you're in seasons of hardship.

New Year's Eve felt like a cruel joke in that first year after Chandler went to heaven. Between the New Year's Eve kisses that I dreaded exploding all around the room as the clock struck midnight, the chatter on resolutions and plans for the year to come, or the drunk girl crying about a breakup in the bathroom, I wanted nothing more than for the night to end. In hindsight, I'm not even quite sure why I made an attempt at going out anyway, I would have been perfectly content at home with a bottle of champagne and *It's a Wonderful Life* on repeat.

I couldn't handle the thought of anything new. I didn't want to face another new chapter without Chandler. And I couldn't fathom the fact that he wouldn't be there for another New Year's Eve kiss.

But that night, I didn't want to be alone. I would have rather suffered in the company of happy people than drown in my sorrow while sitting in the sting of loneliness.

I did my hair and makeup and put on a dress that was new. I didn't feel beautiful in the same way I had while Chandler was loving me. There is something special, some added sparkle, that being in love does to a woman. Chandler used to sing "You Look So Good in Love" by George Strait to me, often. In fact, he sang it to me so often, that I can even hear him singing it now.

Most people make resolutions each new year, but since I was a girl, a friend of mine has always encouraged me to choose a word for the year. Something to focus on and strive toward in every area of my life throughout the new year. The first time she texted me asking if I had thought any about my word for the year this year, my first thought was *Oh, I am not doing that this year, I deserve a pass this once.* A week went by and she asked again, and I told her that I was going to pray about it some and would let her know what Jesus and I came up with while I laughed under my breath.

That night as I lay in bed with the covers pulled up just under my chin, the cold January night freezing my toes, I stared at the ceiling. I went back and forth on asking God what he wanted me to look for in the new year, knowing full well that he would provide an answer, and I just wasn't sure if I wanted to know what that answer might be. My mind wrestled, and I told God so, but eventually I gave in and asked him to place a word on my heart that might help me through this next year and new phase of grief. And as usual, I didn't get an immediate audible response, but when the sun rose the next morning there was a pressing on my heart to be expectant...

And just as I had expected, it was a word that stung in the moment. Expectant? *"Expect what, God?"* How could I expect anything that even briefly resembled hope for my future when the only thing I felt was the heavy burden of my grief. I knew right then and there, God was putting me to work. This new year wasn't going to be a joy ride, it was going to be a homework assignment. And all I can say is, it is a good thing that I liked school...

He looked down at me, his daughter, in a moment of little faith and not believing that anything hopeful or good could come after something so heartbreaking and terrible, but he knew I could handle a challenge.

In the days and weeks to follow—again, as usual when God speaks—Scripture popped up everywhere that matched the word: expectant. I don't believe my God is one to "tease," but I think he can be playful in reminding us of just how great he is.

"A thief has only one thing in mind—he wants to steal, slaughter, and destroy. But I have come to give you everything in abundance, more than you expect—life in its fullness until you overflow!" (John 10:10 TPT)

My counselor had just reminded me of this Scripture around the time my challenge of expecting big things of my big God came 'round. I remember sitting in his office as he read the verse. I smiled at him, thinking I knew just the answer, and said, "Ah yes, the abundant life, made complete in heaven."

He gave me a sympathetic smile as if to say, "No child, it starts *here*."

I left his office that day mulling over what we had discussed again and again and again. Abundant life, more than I expected, wasn't just in the fulfillment of eternal life in heaven, but because I had been saved by Christ and because I allowed the Holy Spirit to make a home in my heart, the abundant life began now.

The abundant life was something I knew could be experienced earthside, but I thought in this season it was surely not for me. And as God usually does, he has far different plans from the ones we expect. And the plans he had were plans to open my eyes to the goodness of him.

125

I listened to an episode from the podcast called *There is More* just a few weeks ago. My eyes were opened to a modern-day miracle, to the goodness of him. A woman who was going blind regained full sight. I was astonished. As I stared at my computer screen of comparatively less meaningful and certainly more mundane Excel worksheets, I had one of those abundant moments where the Holy Spirit fills you up and is made totally available in a moment.

I shuddered. I had been so wrong. Even though I had no idea what God wanted me to specifically expect him to do or to provide, he did expect me to expect that he could, and would, do wonderful things in my life—even miracles.

The Psalms did so much good for me in my days of heavy grief. David wrote of so much honest yearning for the things of God and so much honest grief over his sin and the things of this world. Psalm 25 pushed me to sit expectantly at the foot of the cross daily.

"Guide me in Your truth and teach me, For You are the God of my salvation; For You [and only You] I wait [expectantly] all the day long." (Psalm 25:5 AMP)

"Let integrity and uprightness protect me, For I wait [expectantly] for You." (Psalm 25:21 AMP)

This posture of expectancy was, and still, continues to be a challenge for me. Something I have to consciously evaluate in my life. Years before this reckoning, I made myself a reminder I didn't know I needed.

It was four or five years ago now. I was strolling through an antique shop. It was late summer. I stopped at a stack of antique baseboard trim and picked a piece that was maybe eight inches tall and two and a half feet long. For days now I had had a few phrases running through my head, secretly preparing me for my life to come...

Over and over they ran through my mind, and I knew I had to get them out somehow. Just like it helps to sing the song when you get one stuck in your head, when I get words or pictures stuck in my head, I just have to write them down. I have to make them tangible.

There they ran again as I carried the piece of wood through the shop up to the register...

Get up.

Make a choice.

Chase the promise.

That afternoon after I made my purchase, I stopped by Hobby Lobby, which happened to be conveniently situated right next door. I picked up some paintbrushes and white paint pens. The whole drive home it sang to me still...

Get up.

Make a choice.

Chase the promise.

I knew that beneath the stairs in my parents' basement was where we kept half-used paint cans. Five-gallon tubs of wall and trim color took up the most space, smaller gallons filled the shelves, and tiny quarts of wood stains were stacked at random on top. I chose a wood stain that resembled mahogany and got to work.

I tossed my hair up in a messy bun, threw on a t-shirt I didn't mind ruining, and poured myself an iced coffee. Gathering my materials, I laid them all out on the concrete floor of the basement and stretched out, taking up the space. I opened the side door and allowed the summer sun to warm up the cool concrete beneath me. The sunshine greeted me and spoke once more,

Get up.

Make a choice.

Chase the promise.

I painted the stain onto the wood after sketching my design, knowing most of it would disappear beneath its darkness, but it made me feel better to have a plan. Once that step was completed, I carefully lifted the piece of wood, now sketched and stained, into the sun and let it dry there while I poured myself another glass of iced coffee.

Once dried, I added white paint to a paper plate, and designed some floral edging on either side of where I had placed the text.

Get up.

Make a choice.

Chase the promise.

When I was finished and the piece was dried once more, I covered it in mod podge and nodded my head. The phrase was freed from my brain, and now I had something to remind me of it.

The piece came with me to each place I lived from the time I created it, and it has always had a home where I could see it from my bed so that each morning when I opened my eyes it was the first thing I saw. For years, it became my precious reminder for me to get up for the day since I am not a morning person. It was my reminder to make a choice. I didn't know really what "choice" I had meant at the time, but in this season, I know it means to choose a posture of expectancy and hope. I think there is beauty that with the inevitable changing seasons of my life, that choice will change too. And last, but not least, to chase the promise that God works all things together for the good of those who love him. And just as the choice can change, the promise of God I choose to focus my heart toward can change with it in all the years to come.

Still today, the piece resides above my writing desk in my bedroom. The stain I chose then didn't match a thing I owned, and now it matches my desk and the wood floor in my bedroom perfectly. It is at home here, and I finally know what those words mean from all those days ago. The words that rung in my ears until I dispelled it from my brain the best way I knew how, with just a little paint and elbow grease.

This is another beautiful example of the sweet ways that the Holy Spirit goes before us to prepare a blessing or simply send a sweet reminder.

I am still learning to be expectant, to be hopeful, to know that lightning *can* indeed strike twice because my God controls the skies. God will make good out of all of our sorrows. We need only to offer up open hands, relinquishing our paint and brushes to the true artisan.

Dude 21

*"The sun looks down on nothing half so good
as a household laughing together over a meal,
or two friends talking over a pint of beer, or
a man alone reading a book that interests him."*

—C.S. Lewis, *The Weight of Glory*

$\mathcal{M}$ y work calendar was jam-packed in the weeks approaching Christmas. At the time, the meetings taking up my calendar all day long and the after-hours that pushed on till eight or nine in the evening felt like a major inconvenience, but looking back, I think it saved me some dread. While my heart ached at the thought of what should have been our first married Christmas morning, sleeping in together in our new home, making breakfast, opening gifts while watching *National Lampoon's Christmas Vacation*, which was one of Chandler's holiday favorites, and sipping on Bailey's spiked coffee, I was grateful to be able to push that down just deep enough below the meetings and hubbub that comes with trying to tie up a corporate fiscal year, with a national sales meeting as the cherry on top of the busyness.

It was a Saturday night, just a few weeks before Christmas day, and he would have been gone for six months. Half a year without him was staring me in the face, just weeks away. I could feel its eyes piercing me from afar, just waiting.

I had an afternoon flight to Dallas the next morning, but it was the weekend, and so my lovely sister Ava invited me to our favorite local brewery, Stillfire. I threw on jeans, my favorite black long sleeved shirt, and a camo baseball hat and walked out of my bathroom and told her I was ready to go. This was the best I was gonna do. That outfit had become my go-to wardrobe in those days and still often is…

We arrived at Stillfire, and we picked a picnic bench near the back of the brewery. Ava was planning to meet some girlfriends. I was just there for a nightcap. Our friend Robert who served us often at Stillfire and kept unwanted guests away from our table (thank you, Robert!) headed our way immediately to get our order. I got my usual, a Gummy Bandit, the best green apple sour around.

I didn't say much that night. I think the anticipation of the weeks to come began to press in with the absence of my dual monitors filled with meeting agendas and blue-light-blasted Excel sheets to drown out the reality my life had become. The six-month mark found me there too, pestering me beneath the brewery buzz.

In the weeks before this seemingly regular brewery visit, it had been particularly pressing on my heart to expect God to move in ways that would turn our pain into some kind of purpose. I know no outcome would completely ease the pain of losing Chandler, but seeing some good come from it would have to help, even the slightest bit.

As I sipped my beer beneath the outdoor heater, I read the board of brew names that changed each time we visited, and into my head popped "Dude 21."

Right after Chandler's accident, the boys he worked with at the fire department coined the term "Dude 21" as Chandler said "dude" often and rode Engine 21. The term had even been used when my father-in-law, dad, and I started the Dude 21 Foundation in Chandler's memory to benefit firefighters continuing education as well as sponsor the widows of firefighters for various resources, retreats, and assistance. When the term jogged my memory, I thought, *That would make an awesome name for a beer.* Without hesitation, I looked at Ava and said, "I have an idea."

I waved down our friend Robert and suggested they name a beer Dude 21, and he kindly passed the request on to his manager. When he seemed unsure of how much they'd be able to do, I asked for his email address, knowing if I could just take matters into my own hands and share our story, there would have to be some ounce of good wrung out of that step forward. After all, I was being called to expectancy, so expecting I was.

I learned in this season more than any other that taking a step out in faith, regardless of how small it may seem, holds great power in the kingdom of heaven.

In my eulogy, I reminded the masses that in *Where the Red Fern Grows*, the grandaddy in the story tells the boy that to get what we want, we have to meet God halfway sometimes, stepping out in faith. I took my own advice as I stood in the security line at Atlanta-Hartsfield International Airport the next day, on my way to board my flight to Dallas, Texas, for a work conference.

I typed up the email in the twenty minutes that passed while I waited in line, attaching a few photos of us and the link to the speech Chandler gave at our rehearsal dinner. I sent it off with a wing and a prayer and didn't think much about it in the next few days as my week became busy with work.

Tuesday morning, just two days passed since sending the email, and I shuffled between ballrooms and boardrooms at the Renaissance Hotel in Plano, my arms full of whiteboard easels, schedules, and probably a hot green tea with plenty of honey. In the spare moment I had to check my cell phone, I noticed a missed call and a voicemail from a number I didn't have saved. I put the phone back in my back pocket and carried on.

I tried not to be too hopeful, knowing it could just be another message from that person calling to renew the extended car warranty I never purchased...

When I finally set down the easels I could hardly see over, I reached into my back pocket and pulled out my phone once more, clicked on the green phone icon, and played the voicemail back. It was the general manager of Stillfire, Aaron. He informed me they were going to brew a beer in Chandler's honor called Dude 21 IPA, and they would be donating a portion of the proceeds to the Dude 21 Foundation. They even invited me to be part of the brewing process!

That phone call gave me wings to fly through the rest of my work week.

When I boarded my flight home that Thursday, besides the excitement of sleeping in my own bed, I was so filled up and taken by the sweet fact that my dear late husband would be honored in the most fitting way. A beer was being named after him, at a brewery that used to be a fire station. I squealed on the inside, wishing he could see how big I loved him, and knowing somehow, he felt it from where he stood.

I walked into the brewery on a rainy Wednesday morning in between Christmas and New Year's once again dressed in jeans, my go-to long sleeve black shirt, and my camo baseball hat. I was welcomed in and introduced to the "brew crew," and it wasn't long before I was offered a beer. When I made mention of the time, they pointed to a clock on the wall where every number was five. We smiled at each other and I nodded. "It's five o'clock somewhere."

When I noticed that they were brewing a small batch, I smiled to myself, wanting to remain grateful for their kind gesture and knowing the beer was going to go fast. Very fast. I knew our crowd, and if our wedding was any indication of what the beer release would be like, I knew it was going to be one heck of a party…

The morning of the beer release, I woke up with butterflies in my stomach. It was surprisingly close to matching the anticipation I felt on my wedding day. I was so excited to honor Chandler and to have all the people we loved in one place having a drink in his name once more. I knew there would be absolutely nothing that he would love more. A party, with all his favorite people.

Our wedding reception was the greatest party I have ever been to, and I am not the only person there that night who thinks so, so you can't call me biased! We danced until we couldn't dance anymore. Chandler's dress shirt was so soaked in sweat, that when he asked if we should dry clean it, I laughed and told him to throw it away!

After he passed away, every ounce of joy and celebration went right with him, or at least that's what it felt like. Lamentations said it best: "The joy of our hearts has ended; Our dancing has been turned into mourning" (Lamentations 5:15 AMP).

The morning of the beer release I declared in prayer that the joy of our hearts would begin again and that, as it says in Psalms, our mourning would be turned *back* into dancing.

"You have turned my mourning into joyful dancing. You
have taken away my clothes of mourning and clothed
me with joy." (Psalm 30:11 NLT)

And wouldn't you know it, the Lord answered that prayer— a million times over that night! The brewery filled up with people from all over the state, and we even had some out-of-state guests attend to celebrate Chandler and drink a beer (or two) in his remembrance. That night was the busiest night the brewery had ever seen, and I wasn't surprised in the slightest.

The six kegs of beer they made sold out completely in just three hours, and I still wasn't shocked. Chandler lived his whole entire life loving people and sticking up for the underdog. He was, quite literally, a hero. But you'd never know it by his small town, good ol' boy humility, and that was one of the reasons I loved him the very most. I knew I had to include this story for so many reasons, but mainly because it felt like such a moment of redemption for us.

I want you to check out the total transformation in the Scripture from Lamentations to Psalms again. This Scripture was how we all felt on June 26:

"The joy of our hearts has ended; Our dancing has been turned into mourning." (Lamentations 5:15 AMP)

And this was us by January:

"You have turned my mourning into joyful dancing. You have taken away my clothes of mourning and clothed me with joy." (Psalm 30:11 NLT)

God did what only he could do by redeeming our hearts, even if it was only momentary, as the grief still pulls us way down some days. He turned our mourning into dancing, quite literally, as we danced the night away. All for our precious Chandler.

That night was such a beautiful reprieve from the mourning and the sorrow. It was a breath of fresh air and a reminder that a small act of obedience can go so far in the kingdom of God. That night was also a beautiful example of the marrying of the joy and sorrow that we had felt in those months. It reminded me often in the days to come that the two would reside with one another for the rest of my life. Where there was joy, the sorrow of him being missing from the moment would meet me. And when there was sorrow, I would be met with the joy and the beautiful reality that I will one day see him again.

One of my favorite books depicts this marriage of joy and sorrow quite perfectly, and was (ironically enough) a quote I included in our engagement magazine:

"But if the best of life is, in fact, emotional, then one wanted the highest, the purest emotions: and that meant joy. Joy was the highest. How did one find joy? In books it was found in love—a great love... So if he wanted the heights of joy, he must have it, if he could find it, in great love. But in the books again, great joy through love always seemed to go hand in hand with frightful pain. Still, he thought, looking out across the meadow, still, the joy would be worth the pain—if indeed, they went together. If there were a choice—and he suspected there was—a choice between, on the one hand, the heights and the depths and, on the other hand, some sort of safe, cautious middle way, he, for one, here and now chose the heights and the depths. Since then the years have gone by and he—had he not had what he chose that day in the meadow? He had had the love. And the joy—what joy it had been! And the sorrow. He had had—was having—all the sorrow there was. And yet, the joy was worth the pain. Even now he re-affirmed that long-past choice."[6]

Just as I had been unsure about expecting the good that God could and would do in my life again, that we'd dance and find joy, that we'd laugh without feeling guilty, there we were dancing, laughing, and drinking, joyfully so. We will never have the joy that Chandler brought to a room, a story, or a dancefloor, but I believe there is still joy to be had. Just not his special kind.

God is so faithful to give us those hopeful breaths of fresh air, in the inevitable heights and depths that meet us in this life. Even, and especially, in the middle of our most painful days.

Death Is Not the End

I flipped the Open sign to Closed, picked up my to-go mug of cocoa, and spun my crimson scarf 'round my neck, as I too spun around myself to grab my keys off the café table. As I drew the blinds and turned off the sounds of Bing Crosby, I wondered if a white Christmas would ever appear in my story again.

Growing up we'd be snowed in by November—without question. Mittens came in autumn, and we always had additional winter accessories to add to our Halloween costumes. As much as I had begun to resent the ice, the absence of her made me wonder why I ever left.

But that is the game of choices and change, we get to choose, freedom or blame.

Written winter '17

$\mathcal{I}$ cut my workday a few minutes short. Northeast Georgia was hunkering down for one of our only snowstorms of the season. I knew I would be trapped inside all weekend, and there are few things more lovely sounding to an INTJ like myself to be stuck inside all weekend with gray clouds looming, fat snowflakes falling, and hot tea brewing.

I couldn't wait.

I pulled on my winter coat I hadn't worn all year, threw a scarf around my neck, and set off to the grocery store. I collected items to make roasted tomato bisque to keep me warm all weekend. Fresh Roma tomatoes, red bell peppers, shallots, good EVOO, and some chicken stock filled my basket. I accompanied my purchase with a fresh-baked loaf of sourdough bread and a few boxes of green tea. The breakfast necessities.

As the sky grew heavier and the scent of snow filled the air, I knew I had just one more stop to make. I pulled into the office supply store and was in and out in just a few minutes' time with my arms filled with Post-it Notes the size of poster boards, and a pack of colorful markers.

When I was finally able to finagle the unlock button on my car keys, I threw all of the supplies into my passenger seat. I jumped into the car, grabbed one large pad of Post-it Note tear-off sheets, and adjusted my seat backward so it could fit in front of me. I opened the case of markers and wrote down one of those phrases, like many others through this story of my life, that had been running rampant in my head all day long.

In large red letters I wrote:

How to avenge death?

Tell everyone that death is not the end.

So here I am, after a snowed-in weekend of work, telling you with a grateful heart that this is the truth for those who choose to follow Jesus. I am one hundred percent sold out on this truth, and I am ever grateful that it is our promise to keep. It has been my hard-fought hope on my hardest days and a blessed assurance that will carry me through many more years of certain trial living in this fallen world.

On my hardest days, I have done my best to sit in a posture that is heaven-bound, knowing the glory to come is ever in our midst and the beauty in this life is only a spark compared to the roaring flames of joy and beauty and life that waits for us in heaven.

Colossians 3:1–4 (TPT) ensures this great news:

"Christ's resurrection is your resurrection too. That is why we are to yearn for all that is above, for that's where Christ sits enthroned at the place of all power, honor, and authority! Yes, feast on all the treasures of the heavenly realm and fill your thoughts with heavenly realities, and not with the distractions of the natural realm.

"Your crucifixion with Christ has served the tie to this life, and now your true life is hidden away in God in Christ. And as Christ himself is seen for who he really is, who you really are will also be revealed, for you are now one with him in his glory!"

On Chandler's birthday, I stole away to some solitude at the spa to finish the rough draft of this book. I just wanted to be alone. I wanted to sit with him, just us two, like we should have been. I sat down for lunch, and a few tables away a woman answered a FaceTime call from her little girl. The child sang "Happy Birthday," and I shed a few tears for what should have been.

I did my best to honor him by setting my mind on the things of heaven that day. I drowned my speakers with worship music all day long, leaning into Chandler's new reality and true life with Jesus. I mourned, and I blessed his new life the best I could. I wanted to wallow in hope and peace that passes all understanding on that sorrowful day. I am thankful that I need not understand to have peace, to know hope.

Philippians 4:7 (AMP) says, "And the peace of God [that peace which reassures the heart, that peace] which transcends all understanding, [that peace which] stands guard over your hearts and your minds in Christ Jesus [is yours]."

Holding onto the truth that death doesn't have the final word has been my anchor, and I am so thankful for the peace it has brought me. The last two years of my life have held some of my most beautiful chapters in building a life and dreaming about forever with Chandler. I am so honored he chose me to be his bride.

I was completely his, and he was completely mine in one sense. So much of the beauty that we found in this life together has been buried with him. The beauty of waking up beside him, the beauty of waking up in the night laughing about a joke we told that day, the beauty of his laughter. *That* kind of beauty, the special

Chandler kind, goes with him. But that doesn't mean my life will be deprived of beauty still.

Remember Job. He suffered greatly; God blessed him too. Those blessings didn't perfectly fill the hole left by his grief, but it was a blessing still. It is my job to count those blessings and to seek the beauty in the darkness. The beautiful life we had meant to lead together will never be remade. But there can still be moments of beauty and pockets of joy when we choose to seek after them. God is constantly pursuing our heart with these precious blessings. We need only be still.

"Be still and know (recognize, understand) that I am God.
I will be exalted among the nations! I will be exalted in
the earth." (Psalm 46:10 AMP)

As I move through these new seasons of grief and learn to find new kinds of beauty and joy in my life, even though they're very different, I have had to lean into a few realizations: Life isn't about our happiness, and it certainly is not perfect. I know that these two things may not necessarily come to you as a surprise, but the truth of them is wrung dry when you've learned them by way of grief.

Life isn't perfect. And I don't think it should be. It's in the moments of deep sorrow and unbearable grief that we learn of the ultimate depth of love we're able to possess. It's in the moments of great challenge and trial that we're able to know the gift of perseverance and triumph. Embracing life's imperfection, sorrow, and challenge makes this abundant life possible.

"I am the Door; anyone who enters through Me will be saved [and will live forever], and will go in and out [freely], and find pasture (spiritual security). The thief comes only in order to steal and kill and destroy. I came that they may have and enjoy life, and have it in abundance [to the full, till it overflows]." (John 10:9–10 AMP)

This life's abundance, the heights and the depths, the joy and the mourning all point us heaven-ward. The heights and the joy reminding us that this is just a reflection of the life to come. The depths and the mourning reminding us there is more and "There are far, far better things ahead than any we leave behind."[7]

When I think about my life since Chandler's death, I am proud to say, beneath the rubble of my grief, I have come to find a new kind of humility and strength. At some level, when everything that is most precious to you and the dreams you once held for your future have been taken, you have nothing to lose. My counselor put it this way, "We're playing with house money." I haven't embraced a reckless lifestyle but rather an urgency to be brave, an urgency to live in the abundance we're promised. A new urgency to be honest, even when honesty will bear a hard truth. A new urgency to spend that "house money" on anything that reflects the joy of heaven here on earth.

The most courageous and eternity-minded thing we can do in the wake of death and tragedy is to choose to love in full acknowledgment that it can be, and always is at some point, "taken."

At least temporarily, in Christ, by death. So let us love with boldness and intentionality, until heaven parts us.

> "There is no fear in love [dread does not exist]. But perfect (complete, full-grown) love drives out fear, because fear involves [the expectation of divine] punishment, so the one who is afraid [of God's judgment] is not perfected in love [has not grown into a sufficient understanding of God's love]. We love, because He first loved us." (1 John 4:18–19 AMP)

Sometimes I pray that I always feel close to this pain, just hardly enough so I always cherish more than adequately the things I *do* have. Precious things like time with my parents, reveling in a simple meal with friends, and finding magic in love when it comes 'round, because it is a great treasure, and a true gift. While very, very much has been lost, not *all* is lost, and for what is left, I will treasure for the rest of my days.

This next story was written in the fall of 2017, about my trip to Rome years before on my way to another family vacation. I was just twenty years old. Even then, eternity and the beauty that lay beyond sat with me and held my heart. The Holy Spirit, I am sure, having full knowledge of what lay ahead for me in the years to come.

I remember the first time it happened unusually clearly. Perhaps it's not the most remarkable memory of a young girl's life, but certainly, one worth admiring.

The night was bitterly cold. My hair was pulled up away from my eyes, and my mother insisted that I wear earrings since the occasion of Christmas Eve dinner bore importance for it. My sister, our new friend, and I swerved in and out of the ship to the observation deck to have a look at the stars, not minding the shiver of the Mediterranean winter air. However, looking over the edge of the ship to watch the ocean flare beneath me was too much of a risk in my ebony Christmas gown, so we snuck back indoors.

We hurried through the cigar smoke-filled lounges, passing by people we couldn't understand, listening to *Jingle Bells* in French, and it happened so quickly I hardly realized. The first time I was called beautiful by a boy, it was in a different language, and on an evening that so strongly resembled the glamour from *The Titanic*. You can hardly blame me for remembering it.

We giggled, as young girls do, and the teenage boys with inevitable Italian charm shouted after us "Ciao bella, bella, bella!" (Hello beautiful, beautiful, beautiful!) My previous shiver subsided in a moment, butterflies came, and I thought, *I've been noticed?!*

A few weeks ago, while taking a train to the airport I saw a girl who was about thirteen years old. The same age I was when I was first "noticed." I wondered if she had been or if anyone had told her she was lovely or beautiful today.

When she boarded the train, she walked on with a group of her classmates, and I noticed that she intentionally separated herself from the crowd. She chose a seat near mine, and I saw a sorrow in her eyes that evoked a heartbeat of hurt in me. Her sea-green eyes bore familiarity and a silent, gentle strength—the kind God delights in (1 Peter 3:4).

Although it was her eyes that caught my attention, she stood out for other reasons. A prognosis unknown, but an illness visible.

Her hair was gone, with only a few patches remaining that was the most beautiful strawberry blonde you've ever seen. I didn't know if her battle was just beginning or coming to a final curtain of a long, painful road, but what I did know was that she was strong and seen.

Her book bag was another thing that made me smile. Totally decked out in ribbons and charms, displaying everything she believed in or just anything that sparkled. She was the epitome of a middle school girl. I looked down at my bookbag I was traveling with, and giggled at remembering how much my own had changed since I was her age.

Now, at twenty years old, I only had one charm—a crystal Eiffel Tower I bought just before I traveled to France this past April. I reflected on the lessons I'd learned in Paris as the city of Atlanta flew by me through the train car windows and realized I was on my way to a new country, to go learn more, to go see more, to go hear more languages and see other art. I so badly wanted to be able to show it to her, even if only a moment was allowed for each place.

Paris in the spring. Rome in the winter. Thailand in the fall.

Each place and season was endlessly beautiful, but places and times I wasn't sure if she'd be able to see. In a moment my heart broke and I felt sick. In the small amount of time a train ride provides, I was faced with a decision to bow to the fear of her possibly thinking I was weird and not be the fearless woman I claim to want to be, or fight the fear and step out and be that fearless woman.

I could only do one thing to let her know she was noticed, seen, and strong. As she rose to take her stop, I placed the tiny

Eiffel Tower in her hand and told her to "add it to her collection," and with a gentle exchange of smiles, I knew even more so that she was so, so strong.

Almost daily, especially in our twenties, we are faced with this age-old dilemma to bow to fear or fight it. You have the choice, and no matter your decision, you are going to have to end up fighting for something. You will either endlessly fight the consequences of bowing to your fears (loneliness, insecurity, instability) or you will have to go to war to kill those things provoked by fear.

What may seem like a giant feat can be eternally crushed by the good news that you weren't created with a spirit of fear, but a spirit of power, love, and self-control (2 Timothy 1:7) and that you have been equipped with the armor of God (Ephesians 6:10–18) giving you preparation to go to war with the fear inside you and the loneliness, insecurity, and instability that follow its miserable trail.

Don't bow to fear, bow to the Father and surrender any ounce of unknown to him. In this way, you will have an eternal redeemer, healer, comforter, and friend in the fight.

"But in accordance with His promise we expectantly await new heavens and a new earth, in which righteousness dwells." (2 Peter 3:13 AMP)

A Heart Full of Hope

And I told her as her eyes fluttered closed, eyelashes dusting the moonbeams, "My little nightingale, peace isn't just a dream, for I grew up being chased by doves."

Written spring '19

I have always noticed doves around me. I'd see two sitting side by side on my windowsill. They would wait for me on my car. I would find a pair in a tree while I walked. Even when Chandler and I moved into our home together, there was a pair that frequented our birdfeeder. And after he went on to heaven and I moved into the new home with the chickens, I found another pair of doves there too.

In fact, even as I was writing this chapter, I saw two waddling just outside the window.

It wasn't until recently that it dawned on me, the very obvious symbol that doves stand for—*peace.*

And then it hit me like a wave as most spiritual realizations do: peace, and the one who is our peace, has been by my side, sticking around for years. Peace has been chasing me for all my days through these little birds that always travel in twos, another reminder that I wasn't made to be alone. None of us were.

Peace is in constant pursuit of us. Even when we don't feel like it is.

Jesus is always reminding us of his steadfast love, patience, and grace through the world around us. In whispers through the wind, a fierce thunderstorm, daffodils that bloom just on time, or a pair of little birds, he is constantly breathing his life and his love through his creation, overflowing as perfect endowments of grace to his children who look for it. Like signal fires of his grace, mercy, and peace, the world around us is constantly singing his praises… The katydids, birds, and the breeze singing in harmony, "Holy, holy, holy is the Lord God, the Almighty" (Revelation 4:8 TPT).

It is a gift to know Jesus doesn't just seek you in the secret places or in the pew on Sunday. He looks for you in every season and each moment. Alone or in a crowd of thousands, he will always meet you right where you are. In the silence as the morning sun rises, or in the middle of the bustle of a grocery store checkout line, he is there.

I'll have had less than a year of "grief experience"—heck, less than a year of "widowhood experience" by the time I have written this book. Though I may not be an expert on grief or loss, I do quite intimately know my God and the tender ways he has graciously and mercifully carried me, and continues to carry me, through this journey. In this season of great pain, I have fought to abide with him, even in my seasons of unbelief and hopelessness. I kept digging. I kept sowing. And someday, I will see a harvest.

I suppose that is what this story is for. To show, not what I learned, or how I may have grown, or even to try to teach you how to wrestle with your own grief, but to put on high display the way my God has been *constant* in the storm and how there is always hope—even when I had none.

So, while I may be fresh on the learning curve of grief and widowhood, I am hot on the trail for what the Holy Spirit has for all of us in our most painful seasons. I hope these words point you to the cross, where ultimate healing is found and everlasting hope has made its mark in the eternal ledger.

Unfortunately, these painful seasons aren't escapable—this side of heaven, that is. In fact, here on earth, it is quite the opposite. Here they're inevitable. Maybe even necessary for some in certain cases. It is a terrible truth to realize and be humbled in meeting this realization head on—that this life isn't about our happiness, or dreams come true, but instead it is about our refinement. Making us stronger, more resilient, and brighter in the fire etching us into a perfect creation.

In meeting this realization not long after Chandler passed away, I stuck "The Man in the Arena" quote by Theodore Roosevelt on the front of my fridge with a tomato magnet as a reminder that life would be messy whether I liked it or not. And I can hope and pray it won't get messier than it is right now, but I acknowledge that it can, and if it does, I am staying in the damn arena.

"It is not the critic who counts; not the man who points out how the strong man stumbles, or where the doer of deeds could have done them better. The credit belongs to the man who is actually in the arena, whose face is marred by dust and sweat and blood; who strives valiantly; who errs, who comes short again and again, because there is no effort without error and shortcoming; but who does actually strive to do the deeds; who knows great enthusiasms, the great devotions; who spends himself in a worthy cause; who at the best knows in the end the triumph of high achievement, and who at the worst, if he fails, at least fails while daring greatly, so that his place shall never be with those cold and timid souls who neither know victory nor defeat."[8]

I'd rather be caught sweaty, exhausted, tear-stained, covered in dirt, blood, and tears proclaiming the name of Jesus than be caught on some safe sideline. That isn't for me. That is surely not abundant life. That isn't the heights and the depths. That is not life to the fullest.

In our own journey of healing, we can find the fullness of life, coming to know just how deep our love can go, in losing, and taking up that lesson until heaven parts us, into the ways we love the ones right next to us, right now. I think in the healing we can find the fullness of life by embracing the sorrow fully and the moment's joy equally so. Diving even deeper into the feelings of the flesh and seeking eternity in every one.

In the weeks leading up to Easter, my grief cycle started over from what felt like the very beginning.

The weekend before Easter, I had finally come to collect Chandler's ashes. It was a moment I will never forget. Just before they brought the beautiful oak box that held his body to me, I laid on the couch in my in-laws' living room alone with my eyes closed and I surveyed my memory of his beautiful body.

I started at the top with his sandy blond hair. It was always perfect and never out of place no matter how many times he would brush it or fool with it in the mirror. I remembered his browbone: pronounced, strong.

I looked to his beautiful blue eyes that seemed to change hue depending on what he wore that day. In his left eye there was a brown speck beside his pupil. And in the center of my left eye, I have a white spot in my pupil—together we made the dark and the light.

I thought quite extensively on his lips for reasons I hope are obvious. Then to my favorite spot to rest my head, on the place where his neck met his collarbone. I remembered his chest where the heart I loved so ardently lived.

I traveled down his shoulders, biceps (I used to pray I would marry a man with arms the size of my leg. God answered that prayer, and then some, with Chandler), his forearms, his hands. Oh, how I loved his hands.

I remembered his strong back, the cross tattoo to one side of his shoulder. I worked my way down his back, to his legs, and last to his feet, specifically his toes, which seemed to never stop moving… The last night we shared a bed before he passed away, I kissed the tops of his feet as I walked from the bathroom around our bed, to honor and adore all that he was. I snuggled beside him, beside the warmth, strength, and beauty of his precious body one last time.

I was brought back the moment the front door swung open, and my heart dropped.

The weight of being reunited with his body was like experiencing his death all over again. I wept for hours as I held the beautiful oak box of the remains of my once strong, handsome husband. In receiving his remains, I relived that horrid day in June, and the choices made, feeling angry, disappointed, disheartened, and not hopeful in the slightest. I even thought about changing the title of this chapter, for the lack of hope that existed in those excruciating hours. On that day, and in the days to follow, I was again the girl with a heart full of grief. But nothing stays the same, and slowly, day by day, sunrise by sunset, Jesus tended to my wounded heart once more.

After a few weeks of not touching this book, eating like a bird, as my appetite had been stifled by sadness once again, watching the Bob Ross channel 24/7 for any ounce of peace and relaxation I could find, I found a silver lining. I found myself being chased, or better yet, hunted, by peace once more.

One Sunday, when the sun finally came out from hiding behind the rain clouds, my heart began to reawaken. It is amazing what the slightest bit of fresh air and sunshine can do for the soul. After a walk with my puppy in the park, I took off to the local nursery and splurged on new florals for the yard. I picked perennials, so I knew they'd be back after the winter next year, and I chose flowers that would bring butterflies too.

I spend that Sunday under the sun working in the yard. By the end of the day, my hands ached from the work that had been done. After I had completed what I had set out to do, I threw the shovel down and rinsed the dirt and clay from under my fingernails with the hose.

I surveyed my work and took in a deep breath of the fresh spring air, the smell of flowers and fresh cold water from the hose filled my lungs (you know the smell, sweet like summer). And there I was, filled up with gratitude for the small things—touches of beautiful creation all around me—and I was grateful for the big things too—for springtime, for Good Friday, and for the work done in the days leading up to Sunday, for the resurrection, the smallest bit of new hope, and for finding peace after feeling like all had been lost again.

The work was being done, not just in my yard, but in my heart too. Healing was happening, and for the first time, I could really feel it.

That evening as I walked the dog before bed, my freshly washed hair hung around me, the nearly dry bits clinging to my face as the breeze bent it there. I stepped barefooted from the stone walkway to the blades of grass, relishing in the feeling of it all. I looked up toward the sky that was just barely deepening blue at almost nine o'clock, and I watched in admiration as the leaves in the trees danced, in awe of the way that they swayed together like lovers. I closed my eyes and listened for the katydids to sing to me once more, "Holy, holy, holy is the Lord God, the Almighty" (Revelation 5:8 TPT), and I was grateful.

I think one thing that has been so sweet despite this awfully painful season, is that I have never clung to Jesus like I have now. In some ways, I have never had cause to. But now I see I don't need cause in the first place. I could cling to him in seasons without any pain or trial, and I wish I would have. But now I am. I imagine the woman who touched the hem of Jesus's garment and was healed, and I replace myself, brokenhearted, aching for the smallest touch from him as he passes by in the wind and the waves.

> "Then a woman who had suffered from a hemorrhage for twelve years came up behind Him and touched the [tassel] fringe of His outer robe; for she had been saying to herself, 'If I only touch His outer robe, I will be healed.' But Jesus turning and seeing her said, 'Take courage, daughter; your [personal trust and confident] faith [in Me] has made you well.' And at once the woman was [completely] healed." (Matthew 9:20–22 AMP)

In clinging to Jesus in my deepest moments of despair and sorrow, it has also opened my eyes toward my deep gratitude for heaven, an eternal, unchanging hope. I am indebted to the price

Jesus paid for us to spend eternity in his glory. I am awestruck by his love for us.

I am so grateful that my sweet husband is getting to experience the fullness of life with Jesus by his side. I can see them now, just the two of them, certainly fishing somewhere on the outskirts of heaven...

And so, there is no conclusion, no final dance, no last call for alcohol. Life spins into death, and death into *true life* in eternity. Death is as much a part of our lives as breathing is. In loving and losing, we grieve and suffer greatly for it, but in death in Christ, we become more alive than ever before. While the dead are revealed to *true life* in the completion of heaven, the living are left behind, able to more deeply and intimately know the Lord, and to more deeply and intimately know the true depth of love they're able to possess. It is only loss which can bring forth such a painful yet beautiful revelation.

Hopefully, by now you've gathered that I didn't write this book to tell you all I've learned as a "seasoned griever"—because I am certainly no expert. I wrote this for Chandler. I filled these pages for us. That our story may become somewhat eternal by way of ink and page. Our love, trapped in the binding of this book, on the shelves of homes I'll never know for years and years and years to come.

May the generations know how well I was loved by him, and that I will fight for hope.

I will declare, until heaven parts us, that *even joy* will come in the mourning.

Acknowledgments

$\mathcal{A}$ list of thank-yous that only do a small justice to the ones who have supported me through the most trying season of life:

To Mom and Dad for being steadfast in loving me and holding onto me tight when the tears wouldn't stop, and for every provision big and small. I wouldn't be the woman I am today without your love.

To my sister for being my closest friend and my most patient roommate.

To my mother-in-law, father-in-law, and sister-in-law for taking me in as your own daughter and sister, and loving me as such. From now until forever, you will always be my family.

To Pastor Joey Thompson, for walking Chandler and I through the season leading up to the happiest day of our lives, our wedding day, and for every prayer since his passing.

To Theresa and Bruce at Life Ministries, for counseling me through this journey called grief. You have been and continue to be a beacon of light on my darkest days.

To Marissa Norton, for capturing some of Chandler's and my most beautiful days, and for being such a precious friend.

To every friend who is more like family—this book would double in size if I were to list everyone by name! Not a boast, but a blessing—for your love, support, and encouragement in my darkest hour. You have created small glimpses of fun in my life again.

To Mr. and Mrs. Dale Yark for offering up your cabin on multiple occasions as a writing retreat for Hazel and me. It restored my soul and aided greatly in my healing.

To the Never Alone Widows Team and The Gary Sinise Foundation for providing a place of respite, peace, and healing for widows like me.

To Stillfire Brewing for supporting the Dude 21 dream and turning our mourning, quite literally, into dancing.

To every anonymous precious soul who has prayed, prepared a plate of food, or offered a financial donation to myself or the Dude 21 Foundation, I pray that the Lord would double your harvest.

Notes

[1] C.S. Lewis, Goodreads Quotable Quote, accessed May 26, 2022, https://www.goodreads.com/quotes/21690-there-are-far-far-better-things-ahead-than-any-we.

[2] C.S. Lewis, *The Four Loves* (San Francisco, CA: HarperOne, 2017).

[3] C.S. Lewis, *A Grief Observed* (New York, NY: HarperCollins Publishers, 2001).

[4] Lewis, *A Grief Observed*.

[5] Lewis, *The Four Loves*.

[6] Sheldon Vanauken, *A Severe Mercy* (San Francisco, CA: HarperOne, 2009).

[7] Lewis, Goodreads Quotable Quote.

[8] Theodore Roosevelt, "Citizenship in a Republic," May 5, 1910, Theodore Roosevelt Center (website), https://www.theodorerooseveltcenter.org/Learn-About-TR/TR-Encyclopedia/Culture-and-Society/Man-in-the-Arena.aspx.

THE DUDE 21 FOUNDATION

The mission of the Dude 21 Foundation is to support firefighters in furthering their careers with continuing education as well as serve the parents, widows, and children of fallen first responders.

SCAN HERE
TO GIVE

To contact the Dude 21 Foundation please email us at dude21foundation@gmail.com

Self-Publishing
School

NOW IT'S YOUR TURN

**Discover the EXACT three-step blueprint you need to
become a bestselling author in as little as three months.**
Self-Publishing School helped me, and now I want them to
help you with this *free* resource to begin outlining your book!
Even if you're busy, bad at writing, or don't know where to
start, you *can* write a bestseller and build your best life.
With tools and experience across a variety of niches and
professions, Self-Publishing School is the *only* resource you
need to take your book to the finish line!

DON'T WAIT

Say YES to becoming a bestseller:
https://self-publishingschool.com/friend/
Follow the steps on the page to get a FREE resource to
get started on your book and unlock a discount to get started
with Self-Publishing School.

What Did You Think of *Until Heaven Parts Us*?

Thank you for purchasing a copy of *Until Heaven Parts Us*! I pray it has blessed you in your own grief story or has helped you to better understand the grief story of another.

If it has, please share this book with your friends and family by posting to Facebook and Instagram using the hashtag #UntilHeavenPartsUs.

If you enjoyed *Until Heaven Parts Us*, I would love to hear from you and hope you could take some time to post a review on Amazon. Your feedback and support mean the world to me!

Made in the USA
Columbia, SC
26 August 2022

66134565R00109